Bob Steele's
50th Anniversary:
An Affectionate Memoir

Bob Steele's 50th Anniversary: An Affectionate Memoir

Illustrated by Bob Steele
Written by Jane Moskowitz and Jane Gillard
Photographs by Sandy Hale

Spoonwood Press  Hartford, Connecticut

First printing

Copyright © 1986 by Spoonwood Press, Ltd.
ISBN: 0-939026-08-2

Designed by Laurie Reardon
Typeset by Keystrokes, Lenox, Mass.
Printed in the United States of America

Spoonwood Press, Ltd.
Suite 408
99 Pratt Street
Hartford, Connecticut 06103

CONTENTS

Introduction

It's not everyone who has the opportunity to write a book about someone as well known and as well loved as Bob Steele. We were pleased because, like everyone else, we had been long-time listeners; we relied on him to get husbands, children and ourselves up and out each day.

We knew the project would be interesting, and the research a piece of cake! After all, so much has already been written about Bob, and he has shared so much of his life with his listeners, that we felt like we were old friends already.

Bob graciously gave us a collection of his favorite fan letters, saved over the past several years. After reading these, we realized that collectively these letters said it all, and they clearly came from the heart. It is these letters that form the core of this book. We have added information about Bob that most people are not familiar with, as well as old and new samples from the Steele Smorgasboard of Humor. We invite you to feast!

Jane Moskowitz
Jane Gillard

Bob Steele's
50th Anniversary:
An Affectionate Memoir

It's 5:28 AM. If I can just find that d—d key, I'll be on time!

Music To Your Ears

Cock-a-doodle-do clipclop clipclop clipclop clipclop ruf

> **"** I remember being a young bride, new to Hartford. The first day my husband had to get up for work, I pried open one eye when I thought I heard this ridiculous rooster crowing. Thinking it must have been a bad dream, I dozed off, only to hear the thunder of rapidly approaching horses, hounded by a pack of barking dogs, with our bed in their path! What a way to end the honeymoon! But that day, I started a love affair with Bob Steele that has lasted for 31 years."—*Mary Galvin* Vero Beach, Fla. (Formerly Stamford, Ct.)

For fifty years, the opening theme of Bob's show has been *A Hunt in the Black Forest*. Although one of his most famous trademarks, playing "The Hunt" was not his own idea. It was in place when he took over the morning show from his predecessor, Ben Hawthorne. Aside from not wishing to rock the boat too much as the new guy, Bob decided that all that noise was most effective in awakening his audience at that unorthodox hour of the morning, so he has kept "The Hunt" as his theme all these years.

> **"** . . . my breakfast was interrupted many mornings when you played *A Hunt in the Black Forest*. My wife would stomp around the kitchen saying, 'Doesn't that 'Boob' know there are no foxes in the Black Forest? Those people are hunting stag.' I finally persuaded her to tell you instead of me, where on she called WTIC. You accepted the information graciously, leaving me to enjoy my breakfast.

11

Prior to her death in 1980, my wife wrote a column, 'Saddle & Spurs,' for the Sunday *Hartford Courant*, therefore she was rather well informed on the sport of fox hunting."—*John Lucey* Killingworth, Ct.

All that some hunters ever bag is their pants.

❝Since I've moved my parakeet to a spot next to my radio, every morning at 5:30 she sings as the introduction to your show begins. Bonnie was never much of a chirper, but now I can count on hearing her at least once a day!"—*Margaret Lemrise* Plainville, Ct.

After he had been around for some twenty years, Bob, in a moment of madness, decided to change his musical introduction to David Carroll and his orchestra's rendition of *Good Morning.* The roof fell in. Although Bob felt his loyal listeners would appreciate a change, he soon learned better. After three days, countless letters and innumerable phone calls, he returned to "The Hunt," and equinamity was restored. Obviously, there are a lot of animal lovers out there in radio land.

❝I've lived within a 15 mile radius of Hartford all my life, and I've been listening to you all my teen years, right up to my retirement years.

One of my more recent memories of your program happened

not too long ago when you changed the opening theme of the show. No *Hunt in the Black Forest!* I fired off a letter to you, and I guess others did too. "The Hunt" came back on, and we aficionados of stability settled back with a contented sigh . . .

Almost 50 years, Bob? We can't be getting that old!"—*Kathleen Routhier* New Britain, Ct.

Reginald Dewar, a big game hunter from Marlborough, has been missing for two weeks. It is feared that something he disagreed with ate him.

" In Mass., I lived on the second floor with a lovely, secure outdoor porch.

Every pleasant morning, I put my baby boy on the porch for a couple of hours. 'Butch' (he was very tiny—Butch was a name given as a joke) loved your opening music! He talked very early, and he would say, 'Hear the MOOSTER?' Then he would crow—even after he got on the porch he would continue crowing until he was blue in the face!

One morning there was a terrible banging on my door. There stood my five foot tall landlord puffing, and covered with perspiration.

'It's him, it's your baby—it's Butch! He's my rooster,' said the poor little frustrated man.

It seems that the landlord had a little flock of hens—still babies—when he heard the crowing day after day, he ran to the coop trying to catch not only the world's youngest 'crowing chicken,' but also a hen who dared to crow. The landlord's eyes were red and his bottom lip trembled."
—*Emily Compton*, New Britain, Ct.

" I'd usually come down (from bed) just in time to hear Frank Atwood sign off, followed by the ever magical *Hunt in the Black Forest*. After the rooster quieted down, the dulcet tones of Bob Steele would mingle with the sounds and smells of Dad cooking breakfast . . . Thank you, Bob, for the memories of happy feelings of which you are so much a part."—*Mark Davis*, Springfield, Mass.

Some years ago after decades of playing mild mannered pop music,

13

WTIC hired an expert on radio programming to evaluate their station. He advised them to update the music they played. This meant that some of the "old-time" music that Bob's fans liked had to be all but eliminated. Polkas, another Steele trademark, are now rarely played, and we can only hear two marches per week, on the Saturday show.

Bob loves marches because he feels they have a universal appeal; everyone loves a parade, with its get-up-and-go music. In fact, everyday at the end of his show, when it's time for Bob to get up and go, he plays *The Second Connecticut Regiment March* so you'll step lively through your day.

> **"**It happened here in Greenport, this past Friday night during our Community Band Concert—with 35 members of the Greenport Band present.
> We announced over the address-system that you were doing your part in keeping good music alive, especially the marches you play every Saturday a.m. We mentioned your early a.m. program over WTIC, and told all our music-lovers present to try to catch your marches. . . .
> Our director, Frank Corwin, announced that in your honor, the band would play your closing theme, *The Second Connecticut Regiment March*, and we did."—*Jerry McCarthy*, The Greenport Band, Greenport, L.I.

Before having an argument with the boss, it is well to look at both sides of it. His side, and the outside.

Definition of a music lover: A man, who upon hearing the trills of a soprano in the shower, puts his ear to the keyhole.

Bob doesn't care for much of the newer music; he prefers tunes he can whistle and sing with. However, he realizes that times change, and he does have some current favorites. Bob's feet can't help tapping out the beat of Sheena Easton's *Morning Train*, Julian Lennon's *Too Late for Goodbyes*, and B.J. Thomas' *Raindrops Keep Fallin' on my Head*, to name a few. Some of his fans, however, are not so understanding, but because they like Bob and his show, they continue to tune him in.

"While waiting to hear my birthday,
With ears all full of cotton.
That crazy music you have on
I think is really rotten.

Isn't there a decent record
That we seniors would enjoy
While we wait to hear our birthdays?
Please get one, Bob old boy!"

Francine Towers, Waterbury, Ct.

During adolescence, the music you love is good music no matter how bad it is!

15

Each morning, Bob is sure to sneak in some "oldie" that he knows his long-time listeners will enjoy. Some of these come from his private collection, and others from WTIC's record library. Fans most often ask to hear duets sung by Frank Crumit and Julia Sanderson, a nationally known pair from the early '30s. Other favorites include tunes by Lawrence Welk, Phil Harris, and Sir Harry Lauder's *Breakfast in Bed on Sunday Morning*.

"Over the years you have introduced me to the music of such people as Sir Harry Lauder and Ray Noble. Since they were popular a little before my time, I might never have been exposed to them if it hadn't been for your show.
Recently...I came across a find. An album of Sir Harry Lauder. On the record he's singing such ditties as *Breakfast in Bed on Sunday Morning, Roamin' in the Gloamin, Wee House Mang the Heather,* and *Loch Lomond*...Because of your playing of his songs over the years, I appreciated what I had in my hands and purchased the record. It has since given me many happy hours.
I also purchased a record that had British screen celebrities of the '30's and '40's singing odd bits and pieces. One of the items has Cedric Hardwicke, C. Aubrey Smith and Nigel Bruce singing *Three Little Fishes*. It's a treat to hear them utter such classic lines as 'boop, boop dittam dottam wattam shoo.'"—*Harold Niver*, Rocky Hill, Ct.

"I have listened to you for all your...years at WTIC, and enjoy your program every day. A chuckle the first thing in the morning brightens my day.
But—forty years ago next November, I wrote and asked you to play *The Anniversary Waltz* at about quarter to seven when my 'one year old' husband would be driving to work. Your answer on the air was that you didn't take requests and songs were already scheduled. Can you imagine the shock I received when the tune selected for that time was *You Can't Be True Dear*!! I have never really forgiven you for that, but your prediction was wrong. My husband and I are celebrating our 40th wedding anniversary on November 17."—*Margaret M. Devine*, East Hampton, Ct.

"Do you suppose your people could find a record by Johnny

16

Marvin? I used to run about ⅜ of a mile from school to home at lunchtime to get there in time to hear him sing. My favorite was *On Your Radio If You Hear Him Sneeze, Just Tune Him Out and Let Me Know, and I'll Fix That Big Swiss Cheese.* Then he would yodel . . . I think he was the first singing barber. T'would be great fun to hear him again."–*Ruth Billard*, Woodbridge, Ct.

" On the morning of March 6, 1944, you relaxed your rule regarding the playing of requested tunes and accorded me the singular honor of hearing the song I had asked you to play. The tune was *The Honky Tonk Train Blues*, recorded by Bob Crosby and his Bobcats. My memory is a bit dim now, but I believe that the featured piano player was Meade Lux Lewis.

The occasion? My budding career as a nail salesman at Clapp & Treat, Inc. on American Row, had been cut short by a call from Uncle Sam. Later that morning, I left Windsor by train for Fort Devens, Mass., accompanied by a bunch of equally nervous young fellows.

So the start of the greatest adventure of my life was made a bit more memorable by your kindness that morning."
–*Robert Wade*, Bloomfield, Ct.

Over the years, Bob has become partial to many, many songs. When asked for a list of his favorite oldies, he has trouble choosing just a few. Does his list include any of your favorites?

Sentimentally Steele
Patricia (Prez Prado)
Third Man Theme (Guy Lombardo)
The World Is Waiting For The Sunrise (Les Paul–Mary Ford)
Louise (M. Chevalier)
I Found A Million Dollar Baby
Maybe (Frankie Laine)
On a Clear Day (Robert Goulet)
My Time Is Your Time

At any given moment, when he catches the fancy, listeners are treated to their music accompanied by the warble of Bob Steele's whistle. Whether he chooses to follow the melody or do an original

"MY TIME IS YOUR TIME"

harmonic rendition, it's always expertly done. Bob doesn't whistle as often as he used to because he just isn't as familiar with today's tunes. However, play the right "oldie," and he says he just can't resist the urge to whistle along.

> " Also adore hearing you whistle! I don't understand how you do all those warbles and trills and changes in register in such quick succession. It is all I can do to make a slow, short, wavery quaver."–*Ruth Billard*, Woodbridge, Ct.

> " Mother still loves to hear you whistle along to your tunes, Bob. She says, 'Bob Steele is in a good mood this morning' whenever she hears you whistling along. . .!"–*Patricia Zawacki*, Meriden, Ct.

A Scottish Highlander went to the fishmarket in Edinburgh, accompanied by his dog. The dog accidentally dropped its tail into a basket of lobsters. When one of the lobsters nipped the tail and clung to it, the dog took off howling. The fisherman turned to the Highlander and said, "Hoot, mon. Whussle for your dog to come back!" Replied the Highlander, "Hoot! You whussle for your lobster!"

Bob's singing voice is also not bad. He rarely sings a full song, often clowning around with snatches of a lyric. However, on one memorable occasion, he did surprise his fans with a serious, complete, and delightful rendition of *The Very Thought of You*. During the fifty years he's been on the air, Bob has only done this perhaps five times. The listener who was lucky enough to hear Bob croon on this day experienced a rare treat.

"I had only heard snatches of your singing, and rather suspected your voice would be nice, but you usually clown so much it is hard to figure out how you really sound. I beamed through the entire song enjoying every minute. Normally, I listen to the news and weather, and when the caterwailing and yah-yah-yah's begin, I hang up and go read a book. There are so few really nice voices among all who 'bellar and wail' nowadays, that it was a pleasure to listen to you. In fact, I have stacked you right in there with Nelson Eddy. Not the same, you understand, but of equal enjoyment to me . . . I am still smiling from the pleasure that song, as you rendered it, gave me."–*Ruth Billard*, Woodbridge, Ct.

Did you know that in addition to crooning and warbling, Bob has other secret talents? Although he no longer plays, for a short time he plucked a mean mandolin, and tickled the ivories as well.

Bob's mother felt that all children should learn to play a musical instrument. Bob, as an enterprising nine year old, went to the local pawnshop and for a mere five dollars, purchased a beautiful, gourd-shaped, mandolin. The price was right; (had there been a tuba or a clarinet for five dollars, he claims he would

have bought that just as easily.) Mandolin lessons lasted a year before Bob was ready to move on to something bigger—a piano. His Aunt Ethel, who was a piano teacher, lived across the street, and with her help, Bob embarked on a less than illustrious stint as a keyboard player.

If this doesn't sound to you like a boxer-motorcycle racer, you're right! After one year, Bob wisely traded the piano for a 1920 Harley-Davidson motorcycle with a sidecar. Asked if this wasn't a more dangerous alternative, Bob replied, "The way I played the piano was pretty dangerous. The neighbors who could hear me practicing threatened to break both of my hands."

A man called on a Hartford Insurance executive and said, "All my life I've been unlucky and now I've lost my job. Can you help me? I'll do anything." "What did you do before?" asked the executive. "Well," replied the man, "I played the mandolin with the Hartford Symphony." "That's wonderful," said the executive enthusiastically. "I love good music, and that is my favorite instru-

ment. In fact, I have a mandolin of my own. You must step into the music room and play something for me." Wailed the visitor, "I told you I was unlucky. Of all the instruments I could have named, I have to go and say the mandolin!"

Bob also has a knack for sniffing out the unusual. The infrequent playing of oddball recordings like *Two Buffalos* by Rolf Harris, *Hot Dog Boogie* by the Singing Dogs, and *In The Mood* by the Clucking Hens, cause the ordinary listener to pause and notice Bob's unique brand of humor. One wonders where he finds these things and who would bother to record them in the first place? It takes a man of unusual taste and vision to play them, but Bob isn't barking up the wrong tree. *Jingle Bells* performed by the Singing Dogs is a perennial favorite, and it's not only his human audience who sits at attention, listening to Bob's choices.

> **"** Another recollection from your program goes back 12 years. Our dog was just a pup then, and the first time you played the barking dogs to the tune of *Jingle Bells,* he ran through the house barking like crazy. I had to turn the radio off. Now he is older and wiser, and pays no attention to the record. I know you are thinking he is deaf, but no he isn't."–*Mr. and Mrs. Richard Drake,* Middletown, Ct.

Is this your dog, too? Someone named "D.W." wrote to the Toronto Star's pet advice column with this complaint: "Our cocker spaniel reacts to certain T.V. commercials and jingles by whining and howling. What causes this and how can we correct it?" Pet advisor Dr. Michael Milts replied: "You have a dog of excellent taste and discernment. After all, how else can he express his disgust? He can't turn the set off. Write to the sponsor of the offending messages, and tell him they aren't fit for a dog."

> **"** I enjoyed the poem you read this morning about 'My Mongrel Dog.' That sure is the truth. I don't know what I'd do without my two mutts. Could you please send me a copy?" –*Pat Kane,* Hebron, Ct.

My Dog

He isn't much to look at, that shaggy dog of mine.
You'll never find him standing on a dog show's judging line.

21

No pedigree to cherish, no blue blood in his veins.
I've never seen him pointing at birds near sheltered lanes.

But deep beneath his shoulders a heart that beats for me
Keeps pounding out a message of steadfast loyalty.
His eyes are most expressive, no hatred dims his gaze.
I've grown to love that mongrel with all his funny ways.

He never reckons friendship by coin or fancy dress.
Though all the world may shun me, he wouldn't love me less.
I can't help but feeling how fine this would be
If all could give the friendship my dog bestows on me.

Erik A. Hillbom, North Haven, Ct.

No matter who or what you are, there's something for everyone on Bob's show. From big band to boog-a-loo, polkas to puppies, love it or hate it, it's there, every morning, six days a week, 52 weeks a year, to start New England's day.

"We've been together nineteen years now . . . Although I don't love every thing you play, I couldn't start my day without you. . . . May the dogs always jingle their bells for you, may the hens always be in the mood for you, and may the sound of your rooster always crow."*–Louise Webster,* Weston, Ct.

"Here's a listener who's one hundred today! Let's have that fanfare and a Freihoffer birthday cake!"

"And a Fanfare Please . . . . . .

Bob's Birthday Club has a very select membership. Only fans who are at least 80 years young are eligible, and they delight in hearing "dear Bob" announce their special day to all of his listeners. Those especially remarkable members of the club who have reached the century mark have their accomplishment duly noted by a fanfare played just for them. Some lucky celebrants have had their birthdays announced so many times that Bob seems to know them personally, often mentioning things that he has learned about them over the years. These fans totally delight in the notoriety attached to the yearly renewal of their membership in this very elite club.

"Recently, I wrote and asked you to announce my Grandmother Ida Jane Moulton's 107th birthday . . . Thank you for doing such a fine job. We recorded your announcement as she was not able to hear it via radio, being quite deaf. At her birthday celebration that evening, we played it loud and clear and such a smile broke over her face. When you repeated her name and age, she was very pleased.
One of the family asked, 'How many years has Bob Steele been announcing your birthday?' She thought for a minute and said, 'It must be 27, since I was 80 years old.' "—*Connie Moulton*, South Windsor, Ct.

"I got a chuckle out of this and thought you would too. I am a medical technician working in Manchester Hospital. As I was getting a blood sample from a patient she confided in me that she had just refused her surgery which was scheduled for the next day. It seems that her eightieth birthday was one week away, and she was waiting to hear that she was a member of your Birthday Club. She told the doctor that she was not going to chance missing that honor for anything. Did you know that your Birthday announcements mean so much to people?"—*Susan Pellerin*, Storrs, Ct.

My Get Up and Go Has Got Up and Went!

How do I know my youth is all spent?
Well, my get up and go has got up and went.
But in spite of it all, I am able to grin
When I think where my get up has been.

Old age is golden, so I've heard it said,
But sometimes I wonder as I get into my bed
With my ears in a drawer, my teeth in a cup,
My eyes on the table until I wake up.

Ere sleep dims my eyes, I say to myself,
Is there anything else I should have laid on the shelf?
And I'm happy to say, as I close my door,
My friends are the same, only perhaps even more.

When I was young, my slippers were red,
I could kick up my heels right over my head.
When I grew older, my slippers were blue,
But I still could dance the whole night through.

Now, I am old, my slippers are black,
I walk to the store and "puff" my way back.
The reason I know my youth is all spent,
My get up and go has got up and went.

But I really don't mind when I think with a grin,
Of all the grand places my get up has been.
Since I have retired from life's competition,
I busy myself with complete repetition.

I get up in the morning, dust off my wits,
Pick up the paper and read the "Obits."

If my name is missing, I know I'm not dead,
So I eat a good breakfast, and go back to bed.

In the early days of his morning show, people would occasionally write to Bob requesting that he wish a member of their family or a special friend Happy Birthday. He was always happy to comply. Quickly, however, things snowballed, and so many people wrote in that Bob regretfully had to limit the number of people being congratulated, or he wouldn't have had time for news, weather, or music. Thus, the Birthday Club just for those 80 years young (or older) came to be.

Two elderly ladies met, one said to the other: "What do you do with your time all day?" Her friend's reply was, "Oh, my men friends take up all of my day. I have breakfast with CHAR-LIE-horse; lunch with ARTHUR-itis; I dine with WILL-power, and go to bed with BEN-gay."

You Know You're Getting Old When:
> The gleam in your eyes is from the sun hitting your bifocals.
> Your little black book contains only names ending in M.D.
> You're still chasing women, but can't remember why.
> Your knees buckle, but your belt won't.
> The little gray haired old lady you help across the street is your wife.

Birthday Club members and their families eagerly await the nine o'clock news for they know that its end signals the beginning of the birthday announcements. There is a certain ritual Bob follows as he reads these congratulations. He always starts with the youngest first, building his audience's curiosity until he gets to the oldest, or Champ of the Day. The Champ is then honored with a gift certificate for a birthday cake from Bob and WTIC, thanks to a current bakery-sponsor. All centenarians, and there are between 60 and 70 each year, automatically take the cake!

❝ Thank you for announcing my 95th birthday. . . . I didn't take the cake, but I bought one. Too many 100s!"—*Inez Mahon,* Rocky Hill, Ct.

❝ I wrote to you about Harriet Haynes' 103rd birthday . . . After the fanfare you repeated what I had told you about her sense

39 and holding!

of humor and wondered if she had entered your contest. Well, Bob, she should have. While visiting her on her birthday she said, 'I must tell you my new joke.' A little toddler was playing in the living room with his mother. He found a nickel on the rug, which he picked up, put into his mouth, and swallowed. She promptly turned him upside down, gave him a swat on the fanny, and TWO DIMES came out of his mouth. She was so upset she ran to his father asking what they should do. Father said, 'Give him more nickels.' "—*Sally Conrad*, Fiskdale, Mass.

Club members have their name, address and age announced. Bob especially likes to tell something about the honoree—hobbies, interests or abilities that show how young at heart they are. Sometimes he jokes about a birthday name or address to create yet another small funny, and these remarks are always "off the cuff." For instance, John Strength from the town of Union must steel himself for the inevitable Steele pun, "In Union there is Strength."

Although he won't discuss it, Lee Iacocca's original family name was not Iacocca, but just plain old Cocca. Apparently, the Coccas arrived in the United States late in the 1840s, and settled in Maine. That's where they picked up the I-a.

" I've been mailing my mother's birthdays to you for 15 years. She is blind, and I wanted you to know she appreciates WTIC and especially your program for telling the time. In

28

the morning, you also say what day it is and the date—also helpful as she sends a lot of birthday cards.

She still likes to bake and gets dinner for my bachelor brother with whom she lives."—*M.S. Barrett,* Winsted, Ct.

Another tour group is planning to visit the White House. This one—all senior citizens—will start from Lincoln City, Oregon, and do some coast-to-coast sight-seeing on a bike trip. These folks—most of them in their 60's—will pedal to the President's place. One trip organizer says they won't even have a support vehicle to carry weary bikers or supplies. He says the trip will show that you don't quit living when you retire.

When the eye doctor finished examining the patient, he had to report that the man had double-vision. The patient became angry and jumped down from the chair exclaiming, "Double vision, my foot! You are both idiots."

❝Have your eyes been checked lately?"

"No, they've always been blue."

—*Kay Routhier,* New Britain, Ct.

Anyone with the name of Bertha is singled out further, for unfailingly,. Bob delights in chuckling, "A special Happy Berth-a-day, Bertha." This whimsical wish, however corny, always brings a smile to Birthday Club groupies.

❝... I shall never forget your wishing Happy Berth-a-day to everyone named Bertha on your birthday list since my name is Bertha (I have never taken pleasure in that fact). It has helped me put up with my name. If you had missed even once saying Happy Berth-a-day, I would have been terribly disappointed."—*Bert Davidson,* West Hartford, Ct.

❝Thank you for announcing my Mom's (Bertha Hamilton) ninety-eighth birthday last week. She took the cake that day, but what gave her the greatest pleasure was your special wish just for her, 'A Happy Bertha-day.' Mom is convinced that she's the only Bertha left in the world, and that you're the only one who appreciates a good old-fashioned name like Bertha. Thank you for the happiness you've brought to a very special lady."—*Doris H. Whittaker,* Springfield, Ma.

What's in a name? Associate English Professor Edward Callary of Northern Illinois University has made it his business to find out. He asked a group of first-graders whether they'd rather have a substitute teacher named Bertha, or one named Stephanie.

Stephanie won. Asked why, the kids said that someone named Stephanie would be younger, better-looking, and more fun. They also said that Bertha would make them work harder.

Callary says he can't tell how the kids got that much information from just names. Of course, if the kids could do that much with Bertha and Stephanie, imagine what they could do with some other names that Callary found in the Florida Bureau of Vital Statistics: Skyrocket, Teflon, Lavoris, Etta Apple, and Cherry Pye.

Because times were often tough when Bob was a child, his birthdays were often modest. Gifts might have been necessary clothing, rather than something that would excite a little boy. That is why Bob's most memorable birthday as a youngster was his seven-year-old celebration, when he received a brand-new, shiny red and black bicycle. Can you imagine how he felt when his treasure was stolen just a few days later?

These days, Bob can count on each birthday being special, because he celebrates them with his most important treasures. Children and grandchildren usually get together at the home of his son, Robert H. Steele in Ledyard, for a day of celebrating. Bob will be seventy-five on July 13, 1986, just one day before Bob Steele . . . er . . . Bastille Day.

"One July day, as we were on our way to the beach, you announced that 'today is Bastille Day in France.' My son Stephen, who was five years old at the time, thought that you said it was 'Bob Steele Day.' He exclaimed, 'Gee, they've even heard of Bob Steele in France!' Now every July 14th, I still have a chuckle when I think of 'Bob Steele Day.' "—*Joan Milas*, Meriden, Ct.

"I liked your version of giving out your age. You said you don't tell your age, but you said you were 5 ft. 10. I liked that! I got a real kick out of it. I knew in an instant how old you were. That was four years ago, so now you must be 6 ft. 2."—*Edward Konopaske*, Bristol, Ct.

"Found this poem in the Smith College *Alumnae Quarterly*. It was written by a 90 year old alumna, and I thought it might appeal to your birthday 'boys and girls.' I'm not 90 years old yet, but I think this is great."—*One of your fans*

I can remember when I thought
That ninety years was quite a lot.
But I've concluded that it's not—
Since I've reached ninety.

Before that time you've been erratic
And full of bunk and prunes and static;
There's not much wisdom in your attic
Before you're ninety.

Your judgment's often in reverse,
Your self-control is even worse,
In fact, you almost need a nurse
Until you're ninety.

No need to dread this day, forsooth.
Nay, just keep faith in love and truth,
And you'll be still enjoying youth
Long after ninety!

Grace (Kelley) Tenney, '97

An eighty year old lady invited some friends to her birthday party. "Are you going to have candles on the birthday cake?"

one asked. The octagenarian replied, "This is to be a birthday party, not a torchlight procession."

Daily congratulations also go to those unusual couples who are celebrating 60 years or more of wedded bliss. With so many instances of divorce now-a-days, Bob and his listeners respect the lucky couples who are still happy together after all those years. By definition, people who are in this Anniversary Club are usually in the Birthday Club, too. Some of us never have our names announced on the radio, even once. How wonderful to be so honored twice.

On the occasion of their 80th wedding anniversary, Sam and Annie Loveridge of Langport, Somerset, England, attributed their long divorce-free streak to good food, hard work, and never having a serious argument. At age 99, Mrs. Loveridge still does all the cooking and cleaning. She doesn't quarrel with her 103 year old husband's desire to take it easy. He worked hard as a farmer until retiring ten years ago. Heavy work around the house is done by their eldest boy, Jack, age 79.—London Express

It was their 60th wedding anniversary, and the man of the house was heading out the door. His wife stopped him and said, "John, don't you know what day this is?" "Yes I do," said John. "Well, how are we going to celebrate it?" persisted his wife. "Oh, I don't know," said John, scratching his head in puzzlement. "How about two minutes of silence?"

The Birthday Club has become much more than a clever feature of the show. Seniors know that family and friends care enough to send in their names for announcement. Because of the show, they are often showered with calls from old friends who have heard their milestone broadcast. They become instant celebrities. In a subtler way, they are reminded that they are part of a large, growing group of people who are 80 years young or older. They enjoy hearing what other people their age can do, and take pride in their peers' achievements. Bob's interest in seniors encourages the elderly to continue to be independent, active and involved.

> "I'm sorry I forgot to let you know I will be 87 this February 10th. I'm on the go most every day. I still drive my car and I belong to the Senior Citizens Club in Willimantic. I take care of my car, and clean the snow off so I can get out."
> —*Nellie Wheeler*, Willimantic, Ct.

> "Thanks for announcing my 81st birthday this week. I'm so glad I made it into *the* club.
> Last year, I finally passed the business on to my eldest boy, and now I've got lots of time to do the things I really want to do. My garden this year promises to be a beaut—I've planned extra for our Senior's Center (I'm a Meals-on-Wheels volunteer there).
> My wife and I are planning our usual winter trip to Florida, but we're leaving later than usual. She makes it into the club on October 3, and we want to hear it announced."—*Ed Johnson*, Trumbull, Ct.

It's been a short campaign for Harold Stassen. It began in New Hampshire, skipped the other states, and will wind up in West Virginia . . . Stassen, who is 77 and has been in eight Presidential races, says he's still raising issues. He says President Reagan must be challenged on such things as the use of U.S. troops on foreign soil. And will Mr. Stassen do it again in 1988? Well, he says, "The legend is that many of my ancestors in Norway were still sailing their Viking ships at age 100."

Another benefit of the Birthday announcements is the reuniting of relatives and old friends, and the making of new friends. Often seniors don't get out much, and the Birthday Club provides a wonderful excuse for a get-together.

"For the past 5 years, I've listened to you announce the name of Edna Koehler of Litchfield, Ct. This year, she was 85. Well, my curiosity got the best of me so I wrote to her and had the nicest note telling me about herself, and on this past Monday—which was my 71st wedding anniversary—she came with her daughter and son-in-law to call on me here in Essex. We had a nice visit exchanging our lives.

I'm Edna Koehler, have lived here 71 years, and so I have you to thank for bringing us together. I'm 93, still driving my own car. Never thought Connecticut was big enough for two with the same name. Not too common."—*Edna Koehler,* Essex, Ct.

"Because of your (birthday) announcement, my father received phone calls from 4 old employees with whom he had had no contact in years. He was so very pleased."
—*Mrs. Robert Turnbull,* Barrington, R.I.

"Just a note to say 'thanks' for being responsible for a family reunion. You recently announced the birthday of Valerie Streeter from Cummington, Mass. . . . Fortunately, my sister was listening to your program and recognized her name as one of a long lost 3rd cousin.

Last Sunday, my brother, sister and I traveled to Cummington, Mass. where we spent the day with Valerie. She is the most delightful 93 year old in the whole world, and we had a wonderful visit which included luncheon at the Country Charm restaurant, a ride through the countryside of Cummington and Windsor, Mass., and lots of reminiscing about the good old days when we were kids visiting with our parents.

We plan to see Valerie again real soon as she advised us when we were leaving, 'When you get to be 90, you're living on borrowed time.' "—*Eileen Papushek,* Manchester, Ct.

"Thank you very much for helping my former pupil, David Aston, to locate me. He had searched after hearing my name announced on your birthday program. Can you imagine my surprise when he came in to see me that evening! Did we visit and review the time when he was nine years old, and I tutored him during a bout of rheumatic fever?!"—*Alice Webster*, Bloomfield, Ct.

"Thank you, Dear Bob, for announcing Grandma's birthday. The pleasure that you bring to people like her is better than all the doctor's prescriptions."—*Mary Lou Dunn*, Danbury, Ct.

The minister said, "Life begins at birth."
The priest said, "Life begins at conception."
The rabbi said, "You're both wrong. Life begins when the kids all leave home and the dog dies.
—*Janet Cerbie*, Meriden, Ct.

An 89 year old Dutch motorist had driven 70 years without a single ticket or accident. It was the first time in 70 years of driving that police had even stopped him. But now he's in trouble. He admitted that he's also driven for 70 years without ever having a license.
—Reuters, *London Guardian*

An old man worked on the docks and one day he fell into the water and drowned. There were many people at his wake including some of the older women friends of the widow. They were a nosey lot and one of them got up the nerve and asked the widow, "Did he leave you anything, did he have any insurance?" The Widow said, "Yes, a fifty thousand dollar insurance policy." One of the old women turned to another and said, "And him that couldn't read nor write." The widow stuck her nose in and said, "Nor swim."
—*Matthew Monahan*, Thomaston, Ct.

"The 80 year old man, although still spry and in excellent health, felt it necessary to resist the determined advances of a widow some 20 years his junior. "Mother and Father are both against it," he explained. "You're not going to tell me that your parents are still living?" cried the woman. "Quite the contrary. I'm referring to Mother Nature and Father Time."—*Gladys L. Gage*, Hartford, Ct.

Bob is cagey about pinpointing a retirement date. However, he will celebrate both his 75th birthday and 50th anniversary on WTIC in 1986. He predicts that sometime during that year he will retire. Don't we know all about his predictions, though?

Whatever will Bob do when he finally does retire? Six days a week for fifty years is a hard habit to break. But he and Shirley do have some plans to travel—Bob would like to see America first, then move on to Canada. In addition, he fancies writing a weekly article for a newspaper a la Andy Rooney. Although at some point he won't be a part of our everyday, we hope he will still be a part of our every week. Just remember, Bob's next April Fool's announcement may be for real!

> "You are a rascal. Just when I was starting to feel very bad when you said you were leaving for Idaho, you said 'April Fool!' Don't you dare leave Connecticut and WTIC...."
> —*Louise Johnson*, Manchester, Ct.

> "Ah-ha...I didn't bite...I prepared myself last night, Sunday 31 March 1985 and said prior to going undercover for the night, 'Remember, tomorrow is April Fools Day, don't bite on that Bob Steele's I'm gonna retire routine when you wake up in the morning...' By golly, I didn't. I was ready...I listened patiently...no shock and no surprise ending...I was ready! But I don't know if I'll be that alert come next year...let's wait and see."—*Ruppert Mallach*, Lime Rock, Ct.

A Connecticut physician tells of a colleague who wrote out a prescription in the fashion doctors use. The patient used it for two years as a railroad pass. Twice it got him into Fenway Park. It came in handy as a letter from his employer to the treasurer, to increase his salary. And to cap it all, his daughter played it on the piano and won a scholarship to the Juilliard School of Music.

> "Every morning through 'woe and weal'
> We always listen to our Bob Steele.
> He gives us the weather and the Word for the Day
> And who has the 'oldest' Senior Citizen's birthday.

Someday I'm going to hit the big 8-0;
May live to reach a '60th' with my beau—
But no matter how old and gray we get
Bob will always have a joke that is older yet!"

—*Janette Plassmann*, Moosup, Ct.

"It's not the 'G' in George. It's 'ZH'. Say 'ZH', as in mirage. (MIR-AHZH). That's French, man!"

"Enlightening......"
...... en-light/en-ing

The word for the day is enlightening.
("Be sure you put all the syllables in.")

Enlightening: tending to impart intellectual or spiritual instruction or understanding; a good word to describe this segment of Bob's daily show. The word for the day can range from the impossible to the illuminating, the pedestrian to the powerful, or the silly to the sane.

Just as in the grammar lessons of yesteryear, Bob spells the day's word and gives the correct pronunciation and definition. He uses the word in a simple sentence to make sure its meaning in context is clear. You find you are one word smarter.

"Maybe 15 years or so ago, I was on my way to work very early in the morning, when you mentioned Socrates—a student of Plato and pronounced it So-krayts. I stopped at the next phone booth and thought, doesn't that idiot know it's Sock-ra-teez and not So-krayts?
A short time later after my phone call, you mentioned a learned listener called about So-crates, and you threw in orange crates and grapefruit crates, and I realized I'd been had."—*Jack J. Lappan*, Manchester, Ct.

"I remember a silly ditty my Mom used to sing to my brothers and me after we were all scrubbed and tucked in at night. I never knew what a 'Nabob' was until you explained its meaning this morning. I guess I always thought it meant a good friend, never realizing it describes an important and wealthy foreigner. Thanks for the lesson, and a nice memory from my youth. By the way, I've written the ditty out for you in case you're interested. It goes as follows:

Sure, I've got rings on my fingers,
Bells on my toes,
Elephants to ride upon,
My pretty Irish rose.

So, come to your Nabob,
And next Saint Patrick's Day
Be, Mrs. Mumbo, Jumbo, Jijibu Jay—O'Shea."

—*Barbara Breitbart*, Chicopee, Ma.

Public figures should guard against misuse or mispronunciation of their words, for a speaker's oral or written concoctions often become the meat and potatoes of Bob's English lesson the next day.

Prime Minister Winston Churchill once submitted a draft of a very important wartime speech to the British Foreign Office for comments and corrections. The draft was returned without a comment whatsoever, but where he had ended a sentence with a preposition, some Foreign Office purist had turned the word into a stiff but grammatically correct phrase. Upon reading these, Churchill flew into a rage, and sent the offending grammarian the following note: "This is the type of arrant pedantry up with which I will not put!"

"Humor In The Headlines," a collection of bloopers from across the nation lists the following:

> *Low Necklines On TV Will Be Probed* (Clearwater Sun);
> *Rummage Sale Of Nurses Continued* (Melbourne News);
> *Miami Man Admits Taking His Own Life* (Orlando Sentinel);
> *Man With Two Broken Legs Saves One From Drowning* (Pensacola News);
> *British Policeman Slain For First Time In Seven Years* (Tampa Tribune)

Among the best headlines of the century, according to the Associated Press:

> *White House Advisors Say Nixon Can't Stand Pat;*
> *Speaker At Optimist Club Says Atoms May Destroy Earth At Any Moment;*
> *Miniskirts To Go Higher; End Not Yet In Sight;*
> *Cemetery Site Is Approved By Local Body;*
> *Women's Lib Forces Leading U.S. Concerns To Employ Half Women;*
> *Squad Helps Dog Bite Victim*

Fans of all ages count on Bob to broaden their vocabulary, and the word for the day is a popular feature of the program. Not only do people learn, but they seem to rise to new heights of creativity. The word for the day becomes the inspiration for the would-be poet or author in each of us.

> **"** I hereby offer a suggestion for your Word For The Day. Although I find that people seldom confuse the meanings of the word *bizarre* and *bazaar,* they do mispronounce them with a fair amount of regularity. Permitting myself a bit of whimsy, I came up with the following limerick.
>
> There was an eccentric hussar,
> Who attended a local bazaar.
> He dunked a large goose
> In a thick chocolate mousse,
> And said, 'Please don't think me bizarre.' "*—Harold E. Niver,* Rocky Hill, Ct.

> **"** Your word for the day one day last week, *bade,* the past tense of bid, inspired me to write the following:

It Happened In Eden—
A Short, Short Story

God showed them the fruit on the bough,
And said not to touch it, no how;
If they'd done as God bade,
There'd be little to add,
But they didn't—and look at us now!"
—*Marie Borroff*, New Haven

When Bob was a youngster in the 1920s, radio was just beginning to come into its own. A unique form of entertainment and communication, radio captured the imagination of the general public, and Bob quickly became hooked. Oddly enough, because of the construction of these early crystal sets, the only possible way to listen to them was by wearing headphones. It seems funny to think of Bob and his peers "wired for sound" as today's young people are.

Because early radio relied on the effective communication of words, speakers needed to be very precise. Only accomplished speakers and educated people were able to land jobs in this bold new field. Bob grew up listening to the likes of Milton Cross, Edwin C. Hill and Boake Carter, intelligent journalists and educators who were perfectionists in their speech.

This exposure to good grammar influenced Bob, and when he again donned headphones as a WTIC radio personality, he continued this tradition of excellence. He learns along with his listeners; often they are the ones who provide him with the next "Word For The Day."

> **"** I thought you'd be interested to know that, along with the new "D" stamp, the U.S. Postal Service has also introduced a new word. I noticed it this morning when I went to the Broad Street Post Office here in Manchester. There, taped to the counter front, was the following sign:
>
> D Stamps For Mail
> Destinating
> Within The U.S. Only
>
> Perhaps you'd like to include *Destinating* in one of your 'word for the day' segments. I personally think 'Destinated

From' is perhaps the more correct use of this new word, but I could be wrong. After all, I thought 22 cents was too much to pay for a stamp!"—*Rick Barrett*, Manchester, Ct.

" I have long intended to write to you, to tell you how much I enjoy your program . . . listening to Bob Steele has been a pleasurable pasttime. And I usually learn something. One thing that stays in my mind is the spelling of the word *accommodate*. It was the word for the day, as I recall, and you mentioned that it contains all the C's and M's it can accommodate. I can't count the number of times that memory has come to my aid, and I never have to look up accommodate in the dictionary."—*Cynthia Robinson*, Tolland, Ct.

Bob is willing to bend the rules of spelling and pronunciation to suit his purpose if he's sure listeners or readers are fully aware of his intent. For example, when he was a younger man back in the 1930s, he did a bit of writing for some publications—mostly articles for motorcycle magazines. The by-line for two of these columns were:

Krazy Krax From K.C. (Kansas City), and

Poppings of the Day by Professor Popper.

Bob is the first to admit that these were a bit corny!

I wonder if a Digger who disappears in the Outback might be regarded as a Lostralian?—*Frank Stanley*, Collinsville, Ct.

Do you know that the difference between a "Tightwad" and a Canoe is that a canoe tips?

What does the Bionic Man take for a cold?
"Anti-bionics"—*Ted Schilke*, Middletown, Ct.

The emphasis on proper pronunciation was important in the Steele household. Although each of Bob's boys started with the predictable "kidspeak" of early childhood—one son used to say "hangader" for "hamburger"—he soon learned that Dad would catch him on every error.

> "I thought it might interest you to know that your 'listening appeal' extends to junior as well as senior citizens.
> When my son Matt was two, he frequently used to talk about 'Bobby Deal.' As we knew no one by this name, my husband and I assumed that our son had an imaginary playmate. Then one morning when Matt and I were in the kitchen, I turned on the radio. Your show was on the air, and you happened to be speaking. Matt immediately turned around, pointed to the radio and said, 'Oh! Bobby Deal!'
> Of course, after that, whenever he spoke of Bobby Deal, we knew he was just one of your young fans!"—*Lorna M. Dwyer*, West Hartford, Ct.

A student was asked to tell about the different forms of punishment there were in the world. He wrote, "In the U.S., people are usually put to death by elocution."

The lion sprang upon the bull and devoured him. After he ate, he was so pleased that he roared and roared. The noise attracted hunters and they killed the lion. The moral of the story is that when you are full of bull, keep your mouth shut.

Dr. Boob...er...Bob has been patching up the English language for 50 years. His daily dose of knowledge is an easy pill for all of us to swallow. His prescription is simple: listen, learn and enjoy.

> "Every day I want to see
> What the newest word will be.
> While I listen and I learn,
> I find I've let my breakfast burn.

"WHY IS MR. DIRT IN PRISON?"

Some are plain, some are weird,
And some I fear I've never "heared."
But strange and silly as they may be,
I find I've increased my vocabulary.

So let my toast burn and my coffee cool.
No one will ever call me a fool.
Thank you, dear Bob, for all you do.
When I say it right, it's because of you!"

—*Shirley Bader*, Stamford, Ct.

American author Donald Carroll is back from his latest travels with more examples of how, in foreign countries, a little knowledge of English can be a dangerous thing. English-speakers might hesitate entering a Jordanian tailor's shop where the sign proclaims: "Order you summers suit. Because is big rush we will execute customers in strict rotation." A hotel elevator in Belgrade, Yugoslavia posts this notice: "To move the cabin, push button for wishing floor. If the cabin should enter more persons, each one should press number of wishing floor. Driving is then going

alphabetically by national order." If that puzzles you, how about the Hong Kong dentist who advertises: "Teeth extracted by the latest Methodists." Or the non-tempting Polish hotel menu that says: "Beef rashers beaten up in the country people fashion."
—London Telegraph

❝As one friend said to another: It seems that you had the audacity, the perspicacity and pertinacity to doubt my veracity in an attempt to prove mendacity. Your capacity for voracity and rapacity certainly shows no paucity of pomposity. Enough of this atrocity or I will be put in a condition to force mendicity.

As fellow Missourians altho from opposite sides of the state (St. Louis-K.C.), I also have a propensity for mulishness. Seniority demands respect."—*Edward Moon*, Pomfret, Ct.

❝I was interested in what you told us a week or two ago about a 'Better Bureau Business' someone had founded. A wonderful idea.

I thought you might like to know about a piece of furniture a cousin of mine has invented. It's for high-class executive offices. It looks like a bureau, but the top two drawers contain file cabinets, and the bottom drawer folds out to become a cot. My cousin calls it the 'Bed or Business Bureau.' Anything you could do to promote sales would be greatly appreciated."—*Marie Borroff*, New Haven, Ct.

❝I wasn't fast enough last Saturday morning to get the formula for computing the temperature using Katy-did chirps as the basis.

Thinking about it though, it seems like a lot of trouble to contend with when, for a moderate cost, you can get one of those instruments that hang outside the window with a dial and a pointer. Inevitably, this pointer will be found hovering directly over the correct temperature. This sort of beats counting Katy-did chirps, if indeed you can find a Katy-did, which in Hamden, 99% of the time you can't!

On the other hand, however, if you do happen to have one of these instruments, you could first determine the temperature and then, by reversing the process, use the formula to tell a Katy-did how many times a minute he should chirp!

Up in South Hadley, we have a new member of the family, about 3 months old, and by coincidence, her name is Katy. We have discovered that when she cries—if you count the sobs per minute and divide by 3, then multiply by any number you choose, you will find the computation totally worthless in ultimately deciding what Katy did.❞*—Bob Sadler*, Hamden, Ct.

A whale and a herring were the closest of friends and spent each day frolicking in the deep. Then one day another fish spotted the herring alone and feared the worst had happened. When he asked the herring about the whale, the herring replied angrily: "How should I know!!! I'm not my blubber's kipper.

Perhaps it's from his children that Bob has developed an ear for those silly slips of speech that we don't expect to hear, especially from professional speakers. He loves a tongue twister, funny play on words or transposition, which make the English language so much fun to speak. When a transposition makes sense, and it's his own blooper, you can be sure that fans will seize the opportunity to tell Bob it's his turn to be educated.

❝Several years ago, when Norm Peters was reading the 6:30 a.m. news, you meant to say 'Here's Norm Peters reporting,' but you actually said, 'Here's Norm Porters repeating.' I love this quote from your program because:

a. It is the kind of joke you like, and
b. It was so close, but a tiny transposition turned it
right around!"—*J.L. VanCamp*, East Hartford, Ct.

❝A favorite aunt of mine has a penchant for malapropisms.
She always speaks so quickly that nothing seems to come
out right. I thought you would enjoy one of her most famous
slips.
When she told a friend about my sister Mary Lou's illness,
she cried dramatically, 'Mary Li has tonsilutis, and hos to go
to the haspital.' "—*Carol Lindsay*, Springfield, Mass.

BISCUITS IN A BASKET—a tongue-twister

*I bought a batch of baking powder, and baked a batch of biscuits.
I brought a big basket of biscuits back to the bakery and baked
a basket of big biscuits. Then I took the big basket of biscuits
and the basket of big biscuits, and mixed the big biscuits with
the basket of biscuits that was next to the big basket, and put
a bunch of biscuits from the basket into a box. Then I took the
box of mixed biscuits and a biscuit mixer and the biscuit basket,
and brought the basket of the biscuits and the box of mixed
biscuits and the biscuit mixer to the bakery, and opened a tin
of sardines.*

❝As I was waiting at the bus stop for my little boy to board his
school bus, I heard you reciting a tongue twister about
biscuits in a basket.
I thought it sounded so familiar and then it dawned on me
that I was the sixth grader who had sent it to you so many
years ago.
You said you wondered if I was still a listener of yours—of
course! I grew up with you so to speak. I am married with
two young boys who also, I hope, will grow up with you and
your unique sense of humor."—*Sandra Grant*, Winsted, Ct.

There was a flea and a fly in a flue.
Said the flea to the fly, 'Let us flee.'
Said the fly to the flea, 'Let us fly.'
So they flew thru a flaw in the flue.

This fascination with the proper use of the English language has earned high marks for Bob from the educators of Connecticut. Unlike the old broadcasters, many radio announcers today are not so careful with what they say and how they say it. Teachers know how much time young people spend listening to the slang of the popular scene, and they applaud Bob's efforts to improve our everyday speech.

> "When my schedule allows, I love to listen to Bob Steele. His sense of humor always brightens the start of my day. Not only do I enjoy his jokes, but I appreciate his attention to the correct use of the English language. As an educator, I know that we can all use a reminder now and then...."
> —*David Carter,* Vice-President of Academic Affairs, University of Connecticut

> "Thank you so much for reading the children's essays for American Education Week 1982. The teachers and students alike (of Jefferson School, New Britain) were quite excited on Friday morning when the news got around."—*Denise Roberts,* Jefferson School, New Britain, Ct.

> "I was one of those who applauded when you received an award from Literacy Volunteers of Connecticut. To have a professional of your stature use 'With Literacy For All' to promote proper grammar is gratifying. Thank you for telling so many people about the work of our program."—*A Fan,* Simsbury, Ct.

> **"** I like your daily word and how it should be spoken. I have benefited a lot—I often think you should have been a teacher."—*Adeline Prager*, Hartford, Ct.

This daily dose of good grammar inspires as well as educates. Students look up to Bob as they would a teacher only more so, because he is a celebrity. They are the first to recognize that Bob's mellow mannered style, believability and genuine caring add up to a great educator. Teachers know this, too, and don't hesitate to call on Bob for his help.

> **"** In 1970, I wrote to you about my 2nd grade pupil from a big family who had a very poor self image and was a real loner in my class. She told me once that she always woke up early and listened . . . to Bob Steele. I wrote asking if you could possibly read an original Spring poem of hers early on the first day of Spring. You did just that at 6:00 a.m., and this child walked into class ten feet tall—an instant celebrity. You also wrote an encouraging note to her and sent her your picture!"—*Natalie Dunsmoor*, Waterbury, Ct.

***Have you heard about the woman who was so ambitious for her daughter that she shipped her off to* Marion, Md? *I think she was from* Bounding, Maine.**—*Homer D. Babbidge, Jr.*

> **"** I have been teaching school for almost 16 years, and have come across numerous excuses for students being absent or tardy. There have been the usual illness, overslept, missed the bus, etc. ones. But I had to chuckle when I received the enclosed note today. I thought you might enjoy it too."
> Susan was absent from school yesterday because Bob Steele said Middletown schools were closed!—*Sharon Goodwin*, Bielefield School, Middletown

Here are examples of excuses some teachers receive from the parents of their students:
> *Please excuse Freddie for being out yesterday because he had the fuel.*
> *Please accuse Michael from being absent on January 30, 31, 32 and 33 because he was aleing.*
> *George was absent yesterday because of asore trout.*

Today is:: Tuesday
The weather is: snow

Present today: 22
Absent: Susan
Excuse: Bob Steele said so

Hot Lunch: 14
Milk: 8

Please excuse Betsey for being absent. She was sick and I had her shot.
Joseph has been absent because he had two teeth taken off his face.
Chris will not be in school cuz he had an acre in his side.
My son is under doctor's care and should not take fiscal ed. Please execute him. —Grit

In today's liberal society, Bob's unique belief that there is no place in the English language for profanity is one seldom voiced. He believes that everything worth saying can be said without vulgarity or off-color innuendo. He carefully edits jokes, tiddlywinks and stories that he uses on the air. Fans often send seemingly innocent tidbits to use on the show, and even these don't escape his scrutiny.

But apparently Bob's stand has not diminished his popularity as a public personality. He has the largest listening audience share of any program in the United States.

" Your commentary this morning on the common use of vulgar language has motivated me to finally write you. I appreciated your observations and hope that they will be taken seriously by the language abusers who were listening. . . .
I have listened to your program daily for many years. During all that time, I have never heard you say an unkind or offensive word. It must be gratifying to you to maintain

such a widespread listening audience without having yielded to the poor taste and ammoral attitudes upon which so many other programs depend for their popularity."
—*Adelma Tomkiel*, Simsbury, Ct.

"I tuned in today and caught the middle of your commentary on profanity. I agree whole-heartedly with the position you were taking. It reminded me of a quote I like and wish to share with you: *Profanity Makes Ignorance Audible* . . . . Keep up your high and special quality of work."—*Avi Ornstein*, New Britain, Ct.

When a child asks an embarrassing question, you find that invention is the necessity of mother.

In their own home, Bob and wife Shirley were strict with their four boys, never allowing profanity. This was an absolute law. But Bob is not a prude. His sense of humor will allow him a laugh when he reads something like the following tiddlywink, which he aired on one of his shows.

Police in Mio, Michigan tell about two hunters who support the right to bare arms. And bare legs. And—well, officers say, the two were out in 20-degree weather wearing nothing but guns and sneakers. A citizen reported seeing them, and the two were arrested. It's apparently illegal to be hunting bare in deer season.

Authorities say the two—who were charged with disorderly conduct—seemed to have gone through a lot of beer.

One officer says, "I don't think the deer were in too much danger from these guys."

"...the moral of the story is that when you are full of bull, keep your mouth shut."

"In over 50 years of shadow boxing, I have never been knocked out."

Sports
From the Horse's Mouth

Not everyone can be a convincing sportscaster—you have to know the game. The professional athlete who has that special insight can color his commentary to make it more interesting; Bob is one of those professionals.

Can you picture mild-mannered Bob Steele in the boxing ring, racing a motorcycle or doing stunt work in Hollywood movies? Well, Bob did all three.

His love of motorcycles developed naturally from his bicycling days as a kid. He needed to find work to help support himself and his mother. As an eight-year-old, he landed a job delivering prescriptions for Berkley Brothers' Pharmacy in Kansas City. He had to travel through a tough neighborhood so he quickly learned to pedal fast. Five dollars a week plus tips was all he earned, so the occasional big tipper sticks in Bob's mind. He still remembers Strangler Lewis, a Kansas City wrestler, and world heavyweight champion at that, giving him the extravagant tip of twenty cents.

Bob's passion for motorcycles, which was somewhat unusual in those days, developed into an expertise. The logical thing to do was to turn this expertise into a livelihood. From 1931 to 1934, Bob sold Indian Motorcycles for a Los Angeles dealer, Al Crocker. This job had some fringe benefits. In those days, when a movie studio needed ten extras who could ride motorcycles, they'd call their local cycle shop. That enterprising young man of Steele would send out nine, and count himself as the tenth. In this way, Bob managed to eke out a brief but exciting career as a Hollywood

stuntman. Except for actually being able to ride a bike, the only other qualification you needed was to be able to fall off the bike without seriously injuring yourself. His ability to be a good fall guy earned him each day what he would make in an entire week at the cycle shop. In this way, the small town kid from Kansas City managed to rub elbows with some of the true Hollywood greats like Joan Crawford, George Raft and Joan Bennett.

Movie stars are romantic people—instead of vacations, they are always going away on honeymoons.

President Franklin Delano Roosevelt often told the story of two young men from the Southern mountains visiting Washington D.C. They were walking along Pennsylvania Ave. when they were startled by the roar of motorcycle cops escorting a black limousine. "It's the President!" someone called out. "Wonder what he's done now?" asked one of the mountaineers.

Perhaps it was these experiences that toughened Bob for a career as a boxer, or maybe it was, as he explains, that a certain girl he was sweet on was dating a very tough guy. In either case, Bob managed to jump and jab his way through 70 amateur and professional bouts, until a knee injury forced his early retirement. His keen interest in the sport continues, and he has refereed and announced countless matches.

" I am writing to point out a most unusual feat that you did as an announcer when I was perhaps 10 or 12 years old; it has remained with me ever since.

If I can correctly recall, you were and still are an avid boxing fan and on occasion did some leather pushing yourself. In this particular instance, you not only went a few rounds with an able opponent, but you announced in detail every punch and jab of the fight yourself!"—*Willard Revaz,* Prospect, Ct.

To be successful, a prize-fighter quickly learns that he must always respect the rights of others.

" Although I'm not a fight fan, I distinctly remember something you said on your morning show after you returned from broadcasting a Willie Pep fight in St. Louis about 1950. You were recounting your experiences in St. Louis and reported an interesting, and to me, a revealing story about Pep, who was the world featherweight champion, and what he did on the day of the fight.

You said he seemed to be more concerned about a pair of shoes than he was about fighting 15 rounds with one of the hardest punchers in the world. I forget the name of that fighter, but he was out to win the title. Anyway, that afternoon, Pep's most important piece of business was returning a pair of shoes that he had bought for his little son on a previous visit to St. Louis, when he had fought another contender.

The shoes were too small, and Papa Pep, just like any other papa, you said, was more interested in getting those shoes exchanged than in the approaching fight. And Papa Pep, after successfully swapping the shoes, went on a shopping spree, buying clothes for his son and daughter.

I liked that story and never forgot it—even though, as I said

I'm not a boxing fan. In fact, I'm against boxing, but I'm not against Dads loving their kids and doing little things for them no matter what other pressing matters occupy their minds."—*Morton White*

" Bob and I go way back together—I think to 1937 when he was starting out as a broadcaster, and I was new to boxing. I remember in 1950, I was meeting Charlie Reilly, a southpaw, for the Championship in St. Louis. This was a big fight—Bob was in St. Louis covering the bout for radio. He came into the dressing room and said, 'Willie, this is going to be tough; Charlie's a leftie. I used to fight some, and I think if you keep moving to the right, and fading to the left, you should be ok. Keep your hands high too.' Then he told me he thought I'd win. He gave me confidence, and I did win. I got lucky and I scored a KO in the 5th. I really feel Bob helped me retain my title that night."—*Willie Pep*

A fighter was knocked to the canvas in the 3rd round. Although receiving only a light punch, he did not get up until after the count reached 10. "Whassa matter—you crazy?" asked his trainer. "You wasn't hit that hard. Why didn't you get up in time?" "I was so mad at being floored," said the fighter, "that I thought I'd better count to 10 before I did anything."

A LITTLE GAMBLING
NOW AND THEN

IS RELISHED
BY THE WISEST MEN;
THE WISEST MEN, OF COURSE, ARE THEY
WHO OWN THE JOINTS WHERE GAMBLERS PLAY!

— RLS

Said the slavemaster to the galley slaves who had been rowing for hours: "I have some good news and some bad news. The good news is that you have a 15 minute rest. Now for the bad news: at the end of the rest period, the captain wants to go water skiing."

Why not baseball or football? You would think that one of these would be a more likely choice for a young boy. Getting together with the neighborhood kids for a game in the sandlot next door is as American as apple pie. Instead, Bob chose tough, individual sports. He feels strongly that they prepare you for life, and make you face challenges head on. If you can succeed in a sport that you do alone, you gain confidence and, in Bob's words, you "become tough as steel."

> When a task is once begun,
> Never *leave* it, 'til it's done.
> If the labor's great, or if it's small,
> Do it *well*, or not at all.

When you are getting kicked from the rear, it means you're in front.

As a result of contacts he made as a motorcycle racer, Bob was offered a job as a racing announcer at Bulkeley Stadium in Hartford. Thus began his long and loving relationship with Connecticut. Although he wasn't terribly experienced, Bob quickly developed a style of his own.

" I was attending the auto races one day many years ago, and you were the public address announcer.
I was with a reporter from the Springfield, Mass., newspapers, and he asked me if I had ever met you. I said I hadn't, and we proceeded to the top of the stands to the announcers booth. You were (at intermission) interviewing a famous French race driver and asking him questions, and he was answering in a distinct broken English (mostly French) accent. On arriving at the booth, we discovered you were all alone and had been interviewing yourself!
I enjoyed meeting you, but never forgot that experience and the famous French race driver!"–*Jim Ingraham*, Hampden, Mass.

" My first reaction when I think of Bob Steele is to smile at something he has said or done. Bob *is* funny because he *thinks* funny.
But my lasting impression centers on his professionalism. He has done his show for decades but works just as hard in preparation today as he did back in the '40s. And he agonizes when something doesn't go smoothly just as he did when, as a fledgling announcer, his job was on the line. I have never met anyone, in any field, who had the ability to apply 100% of himself to his job 100% of the time. Bob Steele can and does! And that is the most remarkable thing about a truly remarkable man."–*Arnold Dean*, WTIC AM/FM

In the late 1930s, Bob started his broadcasting career as a sports announcer for WTIC, and continued reporting sports news on TV and radio even after he began his early morning program.

" About 1960, my mother was quite concerned over the fact that I was 20 years old, and had no husband in sight. She decided that I must learn to speak with men on subjects which interested them in order for them to sit up and take notice.
Being a very faithful listener of yours, she passed on to me a tidbit of information on who you favored for the World

Series that year. Needless to say, my co-workers took notice that day, and immediately wanted to know where on earth I came up with that information! I did finally find a husband—without you or my mother, and have been happily married for 21 years."—*Helga Weed*, Woodbury, Ct.

One morning in the dark continent of Africa, a hungry lion was searching for his breakfast. Suddenly, he came upon this family of gnus. "I sure am hungry," he thought to himself. He pounced upon the father gnu and ate him down. Still feeling hungry, he found the mother gnu and ate her down, too. "Boy, that was good," he thought. "I think I'll have some desert." So, he ate the baby gnu, too.

Do you know what he said then? "That's all the gnus for now . . . sports and weather will follow in just a few minutes!"

In 1944, Bob predicted that the St. Louis Browns would win the American League baseball pennant. They were the underdog team but, much to Bob's and everyone else's surprise, they won the pennant! So began his career as a famous sports predictor. Incidentally, that was one of the last times that Bob was right. He has the uncanny knack for picking the right team at the wrong time, and his incorrect predictions have become a source of humor to his listeners. Fortunately, Bob also has the knack of laughing at himself.

> **"**I used to listen religiously to your 6:15 p.m. program, *Strictly Sports*. On one particular Friday, you made *four* football predictions. On the following Saturday, all four of your predictions having been wrong, I tuned in your program as usual, chortling expectantly over what I was about to hear. I wasn't disappointed. You started that program with the music from *A Hunt in the Black Forest*—the part where the dogs are barking. Apparently, you were hiding out in a cave, and an overvoice came on, 'All right, Bob, come out of there! We know you're in there!' "—*George B. Williams*, Newington, Ct.

Fans look forward to hearing these predictions prior to a major sporting event, but many professional teams have been known to shudder at the thought of Bob's choosing them as a winner. It

almost always guarantees their loss. Listeners soon learned where to put the smart money, and some ended up quite well off.

" The memory I have of my Dad is his always saying that whatever Bob Steele predicts in sports, he would bet on the opposite. And I always got something from this—a new pair of shoes, a winter coat, and so on . . .
I don't gamble, but I still listen to you faithfully."—*Ida Ropiak*, Berlin, Ct.

" I remember way back in 1949, 1950 and 1951 when you took a liking to the Tourtellotte basketball squad of Thompson. You predicted we would win the State Class S championship.
You nicknamed us 'The Flying Frenchmen' of North Grosvenordale, but we did not have a Frenchman amongst us! We were of Greek, Irish and Polish descent. This has always stuck in my mind as I was a member of the squad."—*Nick Angelo*, Co-capt. in 1950 and 1951, Quinebaug, Ct.

"There was always so much controversy over your ability to pick a winning team in a sporting event! One day, with a burst of misplaced confidence, you promised to all that if the team you picked didn't win, you'd eat crow. Sometime later you announced that you received a dead crow in a shoebox through the mail. How come you never gave us the recipe you used to cook it?!"—*Harriet Jamieson*, Bridgeport, Ct.

"The good thing about having Bob around is that as long as he's making predictions, mine won't be the worst!"—*Khambrel Marshall*, formerly of WFSB-TV, Channel 3

"One time another of your famous predictions failed, and you honored your promise to ride a motorcycle out of town in a snowstorm at 2 a.m. You brought the motorcycle to the Hartford-Wethersfield town line in a pickup truck, unloaded the machine and rode across the line."—*Tommy Alquist*, Wethersfield, Ct.

"Regarding your well known ability to jinx any team that might have a chance at winning by predicting that they might, I really thought that that uncanny witchcraft only applied to sports picks. Therefore, when the Dow Jones was well over the 1290 mark, and you predicted that it would hit 1300 on that particular day, I went out on a limb with my co-workers to stand behind your prediction. It plunged 18 points! Not only did I make a fool of myself, but it is getting worse day by day. Now that it is under the 1250 mark, perhaps you could predict that it will soon hit 1200, and it might reverse its trend before it's too late."—*Bob Watson*, Simsbury, Ct.

Bob is still an avid boxing fan, but these days he more closely follows baseball and football, and has a mild interest in basketball. Of course, the Hartford Whalers hold a special place in his heart as Hartford's only professional team. The San Francisco 49ers win his loyalty during football season, and the Philadelphia 76ers team is his favorite in basketball. When Bob picks the 76ers to go all the way, Boston Celtic fans breathe a sigh of relief as they feel they are now sure to win.

"Bob Steele is Hartford. His name is synonomous with the city. He is a consummate professional who has the extraordinary gift of never taking himself or life too seriously. . . ."
–*Bill Barnes*, The Hartford Whalers

Each Spring, Bob dusts off and dons his Chicago White Sox baseball cap. Other than the fact that he has always liked American League teams, midwestern teams especially, Bob can give no other reason for his attachment to the White Sox. Nonetheless, he routinely predicts that they will win the World Series.

The stilted language of the Bible is a turn-off to many modern Christians, according to the Rev. Larry Linville, pastor of Wesley United Methodist Church in Trenton, Missouri. He feels he has the answer: Rewrite passages in a language that the layman not only understands, but worships–the language of Baseball. Thus Paul's writings have been reworked for the sports nut in Linville's new book, The Ballpark Version of Paul's Letters. *His pitch is illustrated by this reworking of a passage in* Romans:

> *I give thanks to God for the reports I read on the sports page of how dedicated you are to the game. I swear that I bring up your name in the lineup of my prayers. I pray that my team will play in your town, so I may see you.*

So far, he's struck out with publishers, but that's OK. He's going for the long ball.–Kansas City Times

A teacher asked what the class thought about Beirut. A little leaguer from the back of the room raised his hand and said, "I think Hank Aaron was a better hitter."

George Butters stepped to the plate in a softball game in Casselberry, Florida, and proved why he's called a "power" hitter and a "utility" outfielder. His home run into a utility transformer knocked out the power in Casselberry. A Florida power spokesman says Butters' batted ball blasted a major electrical distribution line, causing a short circuit.

His homer was more of a show-stopper than he needed. It tied the night game at two-two, but then the game had to be called on account of darkness.

Despite his poor record of picking winners, we stay with Bob because he is a winner. Although sports fans may have often asked if Bob even knows who's on first, to us he never strikes out.

> "Last season you picked the Chicago White Sox to go all the way. I thought you were crazy at the time, and I was right. . . . My Dad says that you really know your boxing. I'm not allowed to watch fights, so I don't know anything about boxers. I guess that makes us even."—*A second baseman*, Farmington, Ct.

> "Knowing that everyone has been writing or calling you about Bob Steele the horse, I, Bob Steele, while eating hay in my stall one morning, decided to write and fill you in 'straight from the horse's mouth.'
> . . . Born and raised in Canaan, Ct., I was sent to New York, then to Boston. My winning potential was never met because while racing and winning . . . I was kicked in the knee, which put a chip on it. . . . I was going to retire but this year decided to have some fun and race again. Knowing that I may not run again with the big boys, age and knee problems make me run now only for fun . . . I was well in front of the rest—just as the gentleman I was named after." —*Bob Steele*, The Horse, courtesy *James Blakey*, Canaan, Ct.

"Wanna bet the Chicago White Sox will go all-the way?"

"I enjoy the letters. (Forty to a hundred a day). I got one yesterday from a judge in New Haven: 'Your bus leaves in an hour. Be under it.'"

The Joke's on Boob

...er...Bob

A funny man's greatest source of humor is himself. Bob has certainly proven this to be true. In the fifty years he has been broadcasting, he has repeatedly invited his listeners to laugh at and with him as he tells true stories of silly things he's done. Most of these events are not the stuff of the stand-up comedian; they are stories that could happen to any of us. Somehow, Bob is able to elevate the ordinary to the extraordinary—he delivers the punchline in just the right way to turn that little occurence into a hilarious story.

> **"** To celebrate your 50 years at WTIC, you asked for memorable
> moments, but you wouldn't pay for them. I feel I owe them
> to you for my 14 years of enjoyment of your gentle, clean,
> selfless humor, and your obvious regard and love for all...
> For best story: An icy day in Hartford. You carefully drive to
> the parking garage at 5 a.m. You need to take one step out
> of the car to insert your pass card in the slot. You step out
> and slip on the glare ice, ending up with your body from the
> shoulders down under the car—all in a suit that was just
> flattened at the dry cleaners. An unknown passerby asks if
> you're OK. 'Sure,' you say, 'just checking out the muffler.'
> (Glad you weren't hurt.)"—*Richard White*, West Hartford, Ct.

> **"** Bob Steele was asked to appear in Middletown, as master of
> ceremonies at a banquet. Trolley cars were the main means
> of travel then. As the trolley stopped at Bob's destination, he

69

descended, followed by a lady, young but quite obese.
Bob quickly realized that the downward slope underfoot was
glare ice. His feet went from under him, and he began to
slide. Not realizing weather conditions, the lady abruptly
landed on top of Bob. They slid down the long slope.
When they finally came to a stop, Bob's comment was, 'Sorry
lady, this is as far as I go. You will have to get off now.'"–*Elton
Smith*, North Haven, Ct.

Each of us has felt the embarassment of doing something silly,
or doing it badly, and we'd never dream of telling a living soul the
stupid thing we've accidentally done. But not Bob. He sees humor
in almost everything and gladly shares with 200,000 of his closest
friends the silly things he does. When we laugh at him, we often
are really laughing at ourselves.

"One Saturday, I gassed up at Johnnie's Gulf before driving
to Springfield. I saw you at the bus stop across the street on
the Silas Deane Highway where the Farm Shop used to be. I
gave you a ride downtown and you told me that you had
been given a ride direct from the studio to friends in
Manchester, and they had driven you home. You forgot you
left your car parked at the studio!"
P.S. You are not alone. Before I retired, I used the bus to the
Aetna but occasionally drove. More than once, I bussed
home forgetting my car was in the Aetna parking lot!–*Frank
Havens*, Rocky Hill, Ct.

"You were about to leave on your vacation with your wife—
perhaps in October. You were chatting with a co-worker who
asked where you were going. You replied, 'We haven't
decided. We like a leisurely drive so we'll either go to California or Florida. It all depends on which way the traffic is
going when we pull out of our driveway!'
We laughed then and often, when we are trying to decide on
a destination—whether it is where to eat, which route to
take, or a vacation destination—we laugh . . . and repeat your
line!"–*Gail Karszes*, Somers, Ct.

*A man in a big car was driving down the highway when a
moped passed him. The big car sped up and passed the moped,*

but again the big car was passed. The man in the car became upset, pulled over and stopped. The guy on the moped came up and said, "Thank goodness you finally stopped. My suspenders were hooked to your bumper!"—Brian McNeely, Salem, Ct.

Almost anybody can make a crazy face, wear a stupid hat, tell a joke and get a laugh. The funny man of the airwaves, however, must rely on other techniques to tell a joke effectively; voice, intonation, and mostly, timing are the radio comedian's tools of the trade. Bob is a master in his field.

> "I have long been an early riser and faithful listener to your program on WTIC . . . the continued format of news, weather, homespun philosophy, etc., and especially your inimitable straight-laced jokes with pitfall endings, continue to start my days with many a chuckle or deep belly laugh."—*Sumner Cohen*, Storrs, Ct.

ATSA GOOD ONE!

66 I had to write to tell you that you really made me laugh in
bed this morning. That Alphabet Soup joke was too much. I
couldn't believe it because I was ill in bed with a bug and
was hardly in the mood to laugh. But you know how it is
when you start telling a joke—that ending just creeps up on
you, and before you know it, you're laughing—sick or not!
(And that's no sick joke!)"—*Beth Stein*, West Hartford, Ct.

Fans who have listened to Bob for years have their own mental
picture of how he looks. His impish understated style, his voice,
and his unique brand of humor are perceived differently by each
of us. Some of us, however, are blessed with better imaginations
than others which often work overtime.

66 In the 1940s and 1950s, there was a cowboy star called Bob
Steele. After much discussion and argument, the children
in my neighborhood of West Springfield, Mass., decided that
You were the same person. Many of us envisioned you
wearing a ten-gallon hat and carrying two six-shooters by

your side. This impression stayed with me for many years until I moved to Connecticut many years later, and saw your picture in one of the newspapers. Alas, you looked nothing like Bob Steele, the cowboy star! Old cowboys may fade away, but you and your program have withstood the test of time."—*Judith DeTuccio,* West Hartford, Ct.

" My brother and I were quite interested when you were going on TV on your own program. My brother had quite a shock when he first saw you. You were in ordinary street clothes, and he thought you would appear in a white coat buttoned up to the chin, just like a doctor. He was quite disappointed that you looked like someone that one sees every day on the street, instead of a super star, which he thought you were."—*Beatrice L. Terase*

" One of our favorite quotes in our family dates back to the '50s when Bob Steele was helping us to get out to work and school every morning. This was also the early days of TV. The first time we *saw* Bob, our little 5-year-old daughter piped, 'He sounds like Bob Steele, but he doesn't look like Bob Steele!' She already had her own mental picture of how this familiar voice should look."—*Barbara Hildreth,* Holyoke, Mass.

If you keep your eyes open, you can see Bob as he goes about his daily routine. Just walk down the street with Bob, and you marvel at how many people stop him to chat. He seems to know everyone! It's lucky for us (and Bob) that one fan had her eyes open early in the morning.

" I was walking up Main Street, heading for Asylum St. Just at the intersection of Main and Asylum, a pedestrian stepped off the curb. A truck came by, missing the guy by inches. Thank goodness my reflexes were good then!!! A few choice words were hurled by me at the pedestrian; after which we each went on our merry way.
So would you perhaps agree that your longevity at WTIC can be attributed to me? *You* were the pedestrian!!! To this day, I get a chuckle out of it."—*Viola Saraceno,* Windsor, Ct.

Walking is a wonderful form of exercise—it's sure to prolong your life, unless you try to cross a street.

"Dr. Jones," said the patient from Windsor, "I must say you kept your promise when you said you'd have me walking within two months." "I'm so glad to hear you say that," said the Dr. warmly. "Yes sir," said the patient, "when I got your bill, I had to sell my car!"

Recently, WTIC has aired on TV a series of commercials for its radio station. One particular ad shows Bob ambling over to a hat tree, changing hats, shrugging, then shuffling off. Those of us who know him via radio, smile at this because the personality of the man we've listened to for years somehow shines through in this simple ad.

> "Was dining out and heard the hostess seating a Mr. and Mrs. Steele. Naturally, my husband and I craned our necks to get a look at 'our friend' Bob with whom we have visited almost every morning for the past year since our move to Connecticut. Bob Steele was very attractive, tall, dark, not a day over 35. Of course, it was you! Imagine our surprise when a few days later we saw WTIC's ad on TV. We just knew by the way you walk, the twinkle in your eyes, and the personality you projected that that was the real you. Do you know what? I like the looks of the real you better!"—*An Admirer,* Torrington, Ct.

Bob tells of being in a restaurant and overhearing a boy of about nine say to his mother, "Oh look! It's that man who's on TV!" Most of us have no need to see what Bob really looks like; we just know. However, sometimes a picture is worth a thousand words.

> "About forty years ago, I recall your saying something to the effect that someday, we would be able to see people on a picture, as well as hearing their voice. Of course, you were referring to television. I never had heard about TV, so I expected to see a picture on my radio. I used to get up in the morning and look into the radio hoping to see you! I can remember even turning the radio around and looking in back for that 'darned' picture. Needless to say, I have long since given up the search . . ."—*Lori Shamock,* Meriden, Ct.

74

TV critics tell a story about a quiz show on which a young man was asked to complete the line "Humpty-Dumpty sat on a _____." It was obvious that the young contestant was reluctant to answer. "Come on, give us the answer. You must know what Humpty-Dumpty sat on." "Oh, I know all right," said the young man, "but I don't think I should say it on the air."

Often, what Bob has to report in the morning is serious business like weather conditions, or lengthy like school closings, not to mention necessary like the advertisements he must convincingly deliver. Still, he manages to put punch in these monologues, which makes us sit up and take notice.

> **"** A story you told remains with me always. I often tell people about it.
> You were advertising EverReady flashlight batteries. You always claimed they were very strong and powerful. You told the story as follows:
> There was a bad rain storm that had washed out many bridges. Many people were stranded. You said you took your powerful EverReady flashlight and went out looking for stranded people. You came to a place where the bridge was washed out. So, you took your flashlight and turned it on. You laid the beam across the water; you walked across on the beam, rescued the people on the other side by walking back across the beam.
> I was only about 15 years old when you first told this story—I am now 63!"—*Arthur Kristoff*, Colchester, Ct.

> **"** In giving the bloodmobile announcement about 15 years ago, you announced the various locations, concluding with the location of the State Prison in Somers. You followed by saying that walk-ins were welcome at all locations except the Prison, where there would be no walk-ins or walk-outs either."—*Bill Rafferty*, Shelton, Ct.

A New Englander said to a British fellow: "You have no blood banks in England." The fellow replied: "No, but we do have a Liverpool."

We sometimes think that Bob's the only person in the world who can cleverly turn everyday topics into something humorous. But this isn't so. Although we chuckle when we hear Bob's tongue-in-cheek remarks, there are always those witty people who are quick to turn the tables on Bob.

> **"**I was ever so grateful to you for announcing . . . 'that due to restricted on-street parking around the UConn campus in Waterbury, students were urged to arrive early, use municipal parking, travel by bus, etc.' However, you added that if possible, students should also arrive by hang gliders.
> Please, in the future, refrain from mentioning this again. Our control tower engineers were on vacation, and the glider port was snowed in. As a result, many of our students were forced to land their gliders on the grounds of a hostile campus. The paperwork to extradite them was enormous. The other campus wanted to keep our students for their headcount, in order to bolster their faltering enrollment. One student caught up in the wind currents radioed us that he had successfully landed on the campus of Oxford University in the British Isles. We have an agreement with that institution, which allows him to complete the remainder of the semester abroad. He wishes me to convey to you his everlasting thanks for this dream opportunity.
> Other than the 'mishaps' with the gliders, we had, thanks to you . . . a smooth opening."—*Alphonse Avitabile*, Director, The University of Connecticut, at Waterbury

> **"**I remember the story about the time you closed out your sports show on TV by appearing in jeans and a plaid shirt with a guitar and singing a song! Someone impishly sent you a telegram—collect—which read as follows: 'Caught your act on TV. STOP.' I am sorry that this person did that because he or she may have stifled your career not only as a country singer . . . but also as a clothing trend setter. It could be that we'd now be buying Bob Steele designer jeans and shirts!"—*A fan from Meriden*

My entry for the cleanest, best, biggest joke—the one everyone can listen to . . . Bob Steele.—*B. W. Whitaker*, Somers, Ct.

Bob has been pleasing radio audiences for ten years; unfortunately, he's been doing the show forty years. . . .—*Phil Conte*

Other fans are so familiar with their Man of Steele, that they pen stories in a style reminiscent of Bob's, and attribute them to him. Bob doesn't mind, and he takes his fans' ribbing good-naturedly.

You were going to work on your motorcycle (with a friend)...had an accident with a car. You and your friend were slightly hurt, and went to the hospital. M.D., after examing your knee: 'I wouldn't worry about that knee.' Bob: 'If that knee were on you, I wouldn't worry about that knee either!'
—*Mr. Dow*, Meriden, Ct.

Many years ago, a couple in Mystic Seaport decided they would like to take a vacation cruise. They went down to the wharf to see what was available. Suddenly, they were surrounded, whacked over the head, and dragged onto a galleon. When they woke up, they were chained to a large oar that went through a hole in the hull.

After three weeks of rowing they arrived back at their home port, were unchained, and thrown out onto the wharf.

As they walked away, the wife said to her husband, "Do you think we should have left a tip for the fellow up front beating the drum?"

The other said, "No, I don't think so—we didn't last year."

A 40 year old man was complaining to a friend that his parents were insisting that he should get married. However, his mother took an instant dislike to every girl he took home to introduce. His friend suggested that he find a girl who looked like his mother and closely resembled her in personality. He did exactly as advised. He told his friend who asked, "How did it go?" The man replied, "Your idea didn't work! Now my Father hates her!"—*John DeJohn*, Rocky Hill, Ct.

A very kind old priest was approached by a young lady who told him, "Oh, Father, I believe that I have been guilty of sin every day of my life." The kindly Father answered: "Oh, my dear young lady, what makes you think you have been guilty of sin every day of your life?" "Well," the young lady replied, "Every morning when I get up and look at myself in the mirror, I tell myself how beautiful I am." "Why, that's not a sin, my dear," the kind priest said. "It isn't?" asked the astonished young lady. "No, my dear," replied the priest. "In your case, it's simply a mistake."—*Rev. Robert T. Russo*, East Hartford, Ct.

"Dear Bob,

My Dad always felt that if you can't take it, you shouldn't dish it out. We were always allowed to tease each other good-naturedly, and growing up in my house was a lot of fun!

Listening to your story about how you left your car at the studio and had to hitch home reminded me that the ability to laugh at oneself is a true gift. What easier way is there to realize our own limitations?

Thanks for reminding me that we are all funny people if we just relax, enjoy and forgive our own errors."—Yours very truly, *Edna Clarkson*, Plainfield, Ct.

78

"Whistler's mother would have loved me."

"Just a few calories to hold one until lunch time!"

"It's Friday, and 202¼..."

Bob sneezes and his weight jumps. He tries to keep his weight under the two hundred pound mark, but finds that this is not easy. He's one of those unlucky people who can put on pounds just by looking in a bakery window. This inclination to gain weight causes him to constantly watch the scales. Don't we all know just what he's going through?

Weight watchers of Connecticut know that every Friday morning they can count calories with Bob as he chronicles his current weight. Up or down, Bob tells it like it is. Always explaining the reasons for his weekly weight figure, Bob has been known to blame gains on numerous things. Was it too much of Mama's banana cream pie, or that second slice of bread at Carbone's? Even the slim sisters among us follow this feature, as we empathize with Bob's diet dilemmas.

A giggly woman said sweetly to her doctor, "Can you believe it, I've lost all that fat off my stomach since my last visit here! I wonder where it's gone?" Her doctor's stonefaced response was, "Look behind, madam, look behind."

There is only one secret
To staying thin.
You can't put on
What you don't put in!

Sign on Bob's desk at WTIC:

YOU CAN'T LOSE WEIGHT
BY TALKING ABOUT IT—
YOU HAVE TO KEEP
YOUR MOUTH SHUT!

Gains usually outweigh the losses. As a matter of fact, Bob's wife Shirley once had to take drastic measures to help him win his battle of the bulge. It takes a caring wife to go to such lengths to help her husband stay healthy and in shape, and only a Steele would think to do it with such humor.

> " My happy thought (about Bob) came the day Joan (Mrs. Clinton) Hughes called to ask me to listen to Bob Steele because her husband, Jiggs, and your wife had installed a gadget in your refrigerator that would be a big shock to you when you opened the refrigerator door. If you were tempted to open the door, a voice (shouted), 'Watch it, Fatso!' "
> —*Marge Knapp,* Wethersfield, Ct.

Sympathetic listeners identify with Bob as he wages his war on weight, either by relating stories of their own weight watching experiences, or by finding ways of making him feel better. Bob was left feeling lightly fantastic the day a listener magically reduced his weight from 201 to 92.

> " Bob: Thought you might feel better knowing your weight in the metric system was only 92 kg. Take care of yourself!"
> —*Robert E. Clark,* Department of Weights and Measures, Springfield, Mass.

THE COMMONWEALTH OF MASSACHUSETTS

SPRINGFIELD

NAME OF CITY OR TOWN

DEPARTMENT OF WEIGHTS AND MEASURES

No. 1080

SEALING CERTIFICATE

This is to Certify, *that the following weights*

Submitted by... ROBERT L. STEELE

Address .... ONE FINANCIAL PLAZA - HARTFORD, CONNECTICUT

have been tested and found correct.

DENOMINATION OF WEIGHT	DESCRIPTION, SHAPE AND MATERIAL	IDENTIFICATION MARK	DENOMINATION OF WEIGHT	DESCRIPTION, SHAPE AND MATERIAL	IDENTIFICATION MARK
92 kilogrammes	METRIC	WTIC		ROTUND' SHAPE	
		5.30 -10.00		STEELE	
		AM			

As of Date February 14, 19 83

Robert E Clark

Sealer of Weights and Measures

FORM 63281 Hobbs & Warren, Inc., Publishers THIS FORM APPROVED BY THE DIRECTOR OF STANDARDS

To look at Bob, you would never guess that he has to watch his weight so closely. While he is not a string bean, he certainly isn't that plump "Big Boy Tomato" that wins first prize. But keep in mind that in Bob's day as a young boxer, he weighed in at a mere 147 pounds.

Years ago, Bob found a scale that measured ounces, and was quickly reminded of those boxing days when that same type of scale was used. He was accustomed to a daily weigh-in back then, where his weight was carefully recorded. To his trainer, he had to account for any change, up or down. It seems only natural that Bob continues to monitor his weight, and we, his "new trainers," expect an explanation too. Although most of us would cringe at the thought of telling over 200,000 people how much we weigh, Bob doesn't mind a bit. It's a part of his day, and he's made it a part of ours.

"Dear Mr. Steele,

I thought you would like to know of the great service your Friday morning show has provided for one of my patients. Mrs. X had felt alone and depressed over her weight for many years. It wasn't until she heard your open discussion of how you are fighting weight problems yourself that she began to seek help. Her perspective changed—she didn't feel so isolated, and she even has learned to laugh at herself and her predicament.

Although she's doing well these days—her weight is down a little—the most important thing is that her spirits are up. She swears by Bob Steele!"—*Cynthia H. Adams, Ph.D,* Chaplin, Ct.

" I am proud to say that I have grown up with my 'Uncle' by my side, a man who has become a legend in his own time. Every morning we tune in WTIC for news of the day, weather conditions, school cancellations, good music and a host of other tid-bits which we couldn't survive without. Even the cows in the barn produce their maximum because of your wit and humor.

When I think of Bob Steele in the old days, I remember my Gram and I have to smile. I used to fix her 'scrambled eggs Bob Steele' and she would say to me, 'in old country (Czechoslovakia) we didn't have Bob Steele and I still made eggs with cottage cheese. What's so new about this?'

I have weighed in every Friday with you . . . I even learned to cook listening to TIC. Here are a couple of my recipes for you to try:

When you are overweight, squeeze four lemons, add juice to one quart of water, freeze in ice cube tray in freezer. You can eat *all you want—no calories.*

When you choose to splurge, here is an easy and tasty treat. Open two cans of waterchestnuts, drain, marinate in a cup of wine or sherry for 1-2 hours or overnight. Cut 1 lb. of bacon in half and roll a strip of bacon around each chestnut and secure with a toothpick. Broil until well browned. Set aside. Take 1 bottle of chili sauce. Add ½ of the marinated liquid, 1 cup of orange marmalade, heat well, pour carefully over the chestnuts, and pop into the oven to heat. Serve hot. I love you 'Uncle Bob.' You make my day."—*Joan Toomey,* Hebron, Ct.

Some people go on a diet but most are wishful shrinkers.

Some people are no good at calorie-counting, and they have the figures to prove it.

84

Bob's taste in food tends to the ordinary. He is your basic meat and potatoes guy, although he adores cream which seems to pop up in his favorite recipes. One of his most loved foods, however, is liver, which so many of us dislike, but Bob has adored since childhood. As a kid, it was his job to pedal miles to a butcher to buy hog's liver at the unreasonably low price (by today's standards) of 5 cents a pound. On special occasions, he would splurge on calves' liver which was dearer at 10 cents a pound. His mother, whom Bob describes as a very fine cook, would then turn these into delicious dinners which he fondly remembers.

The polite waiter presented the bill to the patron. Upon looking at it, the patron demanded, "Waiter, there is a five dollar charge here. What's it for?" "That, Sir, is for the chopped liver," was the reply. Said the patron, "Whose liver did they chop, Rockefeller's?"

Some memories of his youth, however, are not so warm. A story that Bob has never told anyone before points out just how tough things really were during the Depression. In 1934, Bob was announcing a motorcycle race in Stockton, California. He missed his ride home to Los Angeles, and was left stranded and hungry with but 35 cents to his name. As Bob tells it, he was truly famished when he entered a local diner. The only item on the menu that was 35 cents, was a bowl of beef stew. It came with bread. Although he was hungry enough to eat ten bowls, he had to content himself with the one. To this day, it remains the best stew he has ever eaten.

To help keep cheese fresh longer, try storing it with some cubes of sugar in a covered dish in the refrigerator. It will keep fresh for weeks, even if it's been sliced. Every few days the sugar cubes will get wet, and need to be replaced.

Given a selection of 31 flavors of ice cream, Bob is likely to choose good old vanilla, or if that's out, chocolate. But on occasion he'll surprise you with a more exotic dessert—like Prune Whip. Bob comments that prunes are a very funny fruit—say the word, and you immediately laugh. At the very least, he can be sure that if prune whip is on the menu, it most likely won't be out.

Prune Whip

Cook 1 lb. prunes in water (to cover) until tender.
Remove pits from prunes and place them and liquid into blender.
Blend 30 sec., stopping to stir down if necessary.
Empty prunes into sauce pan.
Add 1 cup sugar mixed with 1 envelope unflavored gelatin.
Stir well and beat until gelatin and sugar have melted.
Remove from heat—add juice of 1 lemon and 1 orange.
Fold in whites of two eggs, stiffly beaten.
Chill.

(Ed. Those are Wethersfield mosquitoes!)

How much of what foods do you eat per year? According to the U.S. Department of Agriculture, each American consumes yearly an average of:

144 lbs. of beef, pork, veal, lamb and mutton;
62 lbs. of chicken and turkey;
87 lbs. of fresh fruits;
95 lbs. of fresh vegetables;
304 lbs. of dairy products;
75 lbs. of potatoes.

Uncle Bent Steele has contributed the following:

Turkey Dressing

1 pkg. bread cubes
¼ c. celery cut small
4 minced onions
1 egg
½ c. hot water
1 c. popcorn, unpopped
Mix all ingredients together; place stuffing in turkey, and bake at 350 degrees. You will know the turkey is done when the corn pops and blows the backside off the turkey.

Is America ready for a raw egg in it's Orange Julius? The Santa Monica, California-based fruit-juice chain is offering customers what it calls an "eggstra." Posters and counter cards advise consumers, "Just say add an egg, and we'll get crackin.' Employees are wearing buttons reading: "Can we egg you on?" But, to slip in a little added pun, customers who want the raw egg will have to shell out for it.

Although Bob doesn't really cook himself (or anyone else for that matter), he is known to give "original recipes" that he has tried and liked. We are all familiar with Eggs a la Steele (strangled eggs with cottage cheese), and mock crabmeat salad made with parsnips. Recipes for both appear in Bob's first book, *Bob Steele: A Man and His Humor* (Spoonwood Press). However, don't think Chef Bob's repertoire is so slim. Here for the first time in print he gives us two tasty tidbits to tantalize our tastebuds! Enjoy!

Bob Steele's Hartt Beets
(just the thing for the beet generation)
("my Hartt Beets for you")

1 bunch fresh beets
Cook until done. Remove skin and slice or cube.
Don't throw the liquid out!
Use ⅔ cup of the liquid
⅓ cup cranberry juice
½ tsp. horseradish
Butter, salt and pepper to taste.
When ready to serve, heat and eat it.

Chief Bob's Recipe for Indian Potatoes
(serves 4)

Pre-heat oven to 350 degrees.
Butter a one quart baking dish.
Wash four potatoes.
Scalp'em, slice'em, bake'em.

"Some twelve or fifteen years ago, I came home after a week on the road. It was Friday night. My wife said, 'You should have been here yesterday. Bob Steele read a letter from Walt McKain from Russia." The letter had to do with a discovery their scientists had made. It had to do with the detrimental effects that a combination of cottage cheese in scrambled eggs had on the mind . . . something about any predictions the victim made came out exactly the reverse—almost always . . . Dr. McKain had three degrees from Harvard."
—*Jack Daly*, Meriden, Ct.

"We have . . . tried your various recipe hints, and have a suggestion of our own to contribute. On a recent trip to Maine, we found ourselves without cottage cheese to add to our scrambled eggs, and tried using sour cream instead. The result is an excellent dish as good as, or dare I say even perhaps better than, your own recipe. We found that adding a small amount (about a tablespoon per egg) produces the fluffiness characteristic of the cottage cheese recipe, and that adding a larger amount creates an excellent tangy flavor."—*The Perkins Family*, Kent, Ct.

"As for *The Little Red Hen*—surely you must know that this story was proven false in 1873 by the well-known scientist, Dr. Surgical Steele, who demonstrated, by experiment, that a hen is utterly incapable of making bread. He gave a little red hen all the necessary utensils and ingredients for making a plain, white loaf and told her to go ahead and do as her relative was reported to have done. Well, in a few minutes, the hen had made a pretty sorry mess of things, and had herself ended up in the dough pan, covered with flour. Dr. Steele, being a frugal man and unwilling to waste all the materials, proceeded to pour in the yeast—which, in a manner of speaking, gave rise to what is known in some circles as chicken and dumplings. (Dr. Steele later invented the crowbar, but he had some difficulty getting the crows to patronize it.)"—*George D. Vaill*, Colebrook, Ct.

You can't blame food producers for trying to sell their products. But some of the uses they've cooked up for their food have caused more than one stomach to turn among those reading their press releases. Knight-Ridder News Service food writer Jane Snow has now announced the most tastelessly creative recipes she saw in 1983. The American Egg Board gets a crack at honors for its recipe for eggs poached in canned tomato soup. From a cookware manufacturer came "Prune Puree" sandwich spread. A sauerkraut manufacturer supplied the recipe for "egg foo kraut." A fruit cocktail maker tried to cash in on the Mexican food craze with a recipe for a tostada with beans, diced chicken, onions, lettuce and cheese, topped off with a generous helping of fruit cocktail. The Gatorade people offered a "great-tasting alternative to cold-weather beverages like coffee, cocoa and hot cider"—hot Gatorade. Then there was fried spaghetti pie, peanut-butter meat loaf, popcorn meat loaf, and from Pacific Coast Canned Pear Service, meatballs simmered with canned pears.

A frugal housewife asked the grocer how much he got for cracked eggs. He said, "Half price." She replied, "Okay, crack me a dozen!"

While world reknown chefs seem to manage without Bob's help, local cooks find Bob's taste in food delectable. Listeners love to try his recipes and will go to any length to be sure they get them as he reads them over the radio. While his recipes may not be hazardous to our health, writing them down can be.

"Five or six years ago, I was driving North on Route 91 to Northfield, Mass., and you were going to give a recipe for mock crabmeat salad made with shredded parsnips. I decided to stop the car and get a paper and pencil out and write it down, as my mother likes crabmeat salad.
After you gave the recipe, you were talking about the fact

that you hoped people had gotten a piece of paper and pencil and written it down—'But of course you wouldn't do that if you were driving your car.' That is what I had just done! My children were in the car with me and properly chastised me!"—*Enid La Fleur,* Windsor, Ct.

However, sometimes a listener won't be happy with the results of Bob's concoctions. A fan who liked cream in his coffee tried to short-cut Bob's famous recipe for coffee made with club soda and cream by making it with cream soda. Needless to say, he was very disappointed with the results, and was quick to let Bob know that the cream soda just didn't work the way it was supposed to. Let this be a lesson to those who like to try Bob's recipes. Don't tamper with perfection.

A guy walked into a donut shop carrying a thermos bottle. He asked the manager how much coffee would it hold. The manager said six cups. "OK," said the man, "give me 2 regular, 2 with sugar, and 2 black."—*Fred Lindahl,* West Yarmouth, Mass.

I SEE YOU OUT THERE! THAT WAS YOUR SECOND CRULLER!

*College food can be more than mystery meat from the cafeteria—
or another Mcburger to grease-stain your corduroys. At Loyola
University in New Orleans, well-dressed students dine on the
finest the city's great chefs can produce. White-gloved waiters
serve, while a string quartet plays chamber music.*

*One chef says his offering for this meal-of-the-month club
would cost up to 75 dollars a person at his hotel. But at Loyola,
it's free—just part of the meal-ticket plan.*

*The school figures that being well-fed is part of being well-
rounded.*

When he has to, Bob puts himself on a diet which is very basic;
he cuts out sweets, breads, butter and potatoes, and is on his
way to a slimmer Steele.

He believes in three meals a day; when he diets, they just
become very simple. For breakfast, he'll have a scant ¾ cup of
coffee and just a small slice of Shirley's coffee cake. (This is a treat
he can't resist.) Lunch is cottage cheese and pineapple. Dinner
might consist of meat, salad and a vegetable. Desserts are a no-no.

Shirley Steele's Sour Cream Coffee Cake

½ c. butter
1 c. granulated sugar
2 eggs
2 c. sifted all purpose flour
1 tsp. soda
1 tsp. baking powder
½ tsp. salt
1 c. cultured sour cream
1 tsp. vanilla

For the topping, combine:
¼ c. white sugar
⅓ c. brown sugar, firmly packed
1 tsp. cinnamon
1 c. pecans, finely chopped
Preheat oven to 325 degrees. Cream butter and sugar. Add
eggs, one at a time, beating well. Sift dry ingredients together.
Add to creamed mixture alternately with sour cream, begin-

ning and ending with flour. Stir in vanilla. Pour half of the batter into a buttered 9x9 inch baking pan; cover with half of the nut topping. Pour remaining batter over the filling, and top with the rest of the nut mixture. Bake approximately 40 minutes.

Bob claims that one thing that makes Shirley's coffee cake so special is her painstaking attention to the nuts. She carefully picks over the nut meats to be absolutely sure that the shell is completely removed. The reason? Bob says that "shells in nuts are like sand in spinach."

A young minister, in the early days of his first parish, was obliged to call upon the widow of an eccentric man who had just died. Standing before the open casket consoling the widow, he said, "I know this must be a very hard blow, Mrs. Blank. But we must remember that what we see here is only husk—only the shell. The nut has gone to heaven.

A pastor got this note accompanying a box of goodies, addressed to him and his wife from an old lady in the parish: "Dear Pastor, Knowing that you do not eat sweets, I am sending candy to your wife, and nuts to you."

The Hartford area boasts of many fine restaurants. In addition to continental cuisine, area diners can sample foods of many different cultures. Bob and Shirley frequently eat out and over the years have picked their favorite spots. The shish-ka-bob at Adajian's (Hartford) and the roast beef at The Hawthorne (Berlin) are two meals he especially enjoys. Bob is also particularly fond of Italian food, and he often eats at Carbone's (Hartford), La Trattoria (Canton) and Leon's (New Haven).

" No one really knows what brought Bob Steele to Hartford; some think it was WTIC, but we prefer to think it was to dine at Carbone's.
Over the years, we have watched Bob's family grow. His weight was like the stock market. It had it's ups and downs. A love for the finer things in life is reflected in the way he dines.

The Carbone family salutes you, Bob; it's a privilege to serve a friend."—*Guy and Carl Carbone*, Carbone's Ristorante, Hartford, Ct.

One of Britain's most carefree private clubs specializes in serving fourth-rate food. It may be warmed-over macaroni and cheese one evening, and a dubious stew another, at the club named "School Dinners." It's an attempt to bring back those fun times in boarding school dining halls. Diners get insulted by the head-master and have to ask permission to go to the bathroom. But they get to play pranks. If they're too naughty, however, they get caned.—Entrepeneur Magaine

A couple were sitting at a table in a restaurant. As the waiter across the room glanced at them, he saw the man slide off the chair, down under the table. The lady did not seem to pay atten-tion, so the waiter went over and spoke to her saying, "Lady, do you know that your husband just slid off his chair and under the table?" She said, "No, my husband just came in the front door."—William Harding

Despite the fine meals that Bob enjoys in restaurants, his wife Shirley's table remains his favorite place to dine. The specialties of the house are banana cream pie and sunshine cake. Bob claims that the Swede in Shirley makes her measure in pinches and handfuls, rather than tablespoons and cups. Those of us who are not as creative need precise instructions, and Shirley Steele has done her best to come up with the following:

Sunshine Cake

Beat 4 egg yolks and 3 tbls. cold water together; add 1½ c. sugar gradually. Beat well. Add ½ c. boiling water and beat until foamy. Sift 3 times 1½ c. cake flour, 1 tsp. baking powder, and ¼ tsp. salt. Add egg yolks. Beat well. Add 1 tsp. vanilla or almond extract.

Beat egg whites with ½ tsp. cream of tartar until stiff, and fold into the mixture. Bake about 1 hour at 325 degrees. Use an ungreased tube pan. Be sure you invert the cake in its pan to cool.

"This morning, during construction of my breakfast, I was unable to locate any cottage cheese (with which to make your famous scrambled eggs)... I selected a substitute which just might attain a portion of the fame of your specialty. ...
There is on the market a bottled salad dressing called Creamy Bacon... Belonging to the '3D' school of home cooking, i.e., a Dash, a Dribble, and a Dollop, I reckon that I added one Dollop of Creamy Bacon dressing to the two eggs in the bowl before beating with a fork. (By actual measure, a dollop is the exact equivalent of a teaspoon.)... History was made in my kitchen this a.m...."–*Bob Wade*, Bloomfield, Ct.

"When I called my Grandmother to get her recipe for mince-meat, she was more than happy to comply.
Since you mention how hard it is to get an exact recipe from your wife, I thought you'd appreciate reading the recipe my Grandmother gave me. I had to call her back three times to get it right!"–*A Loyal Fan*, Hamden, Ct.

Grandmother's Mincemeat

About 3 cupfuls of meat in a heavy saucepan
About ½ cup of beef suet
4 cupfuls of chopped apples
only 1 cup sugar
I usually throw in about 3 cups of dark brown sugar, softened
with apple juice (if you want to use it up)
maybe 1 more cup apples, chopped
2-3 cups raisins
1 + cups currents
2 large containers mixed fruit
1 c. vinegar
½ c. water
some spices: allspice, cloves, cinnamon, nutmeg

Cook slowly 1½ hours (off and on—I wait until I'm in the
kitchen again). Let set between cookings.
Add some cooking wine, if you have any. Let set.
At this cooking, add 1 orange peel and ½ lemon peel, ground
fine.
Cook until tender.
Taste and adjust. I sometimes add ½ or so jar marmalade,
½ jar peach marmalade (if available)... I often add the rem-
nants of a grape jelly jar, too.
If it tastes good, add 1 c. brandy on top and let set overnight.

If you want to get fat, don't fast.
If you want to get thin, don't eat—fast.

*A fellow figured he would cash in on holiday demand, and
crossed a turkey with an ostrich. He figured he'd get something with enormous drumsticks. Instead, he came up with a
very strange bird that just ran over and buried it's head in
the mashed potatoes.*

You might wonder if Bob exercises to help keep his weight down.
The answer is no. As a boxer in training, he used to follow a strict
exercise regimen that included a five mile run, and a 2 hour work-
out in the gym. But that was when boxing was his business. These
days, his exercise program is quite a bit shorter. Although he does

bike some, he claims that his main form of daily exercise is getting dressed. In fact, the only reason he has never installed an automatic garage door opener is because he feels he gets a work-out by opening and closing it!

Despite his light-hearted ribbing, we know that Bob understands the importance of diet and exercise for our health. With this humorous approach, we are painlessly encouraged to stay in shape.

"In days of yore when I was thin,
I never thought what I put in.
Chocolate cake, donuts, and lemon cream pie
I'd eat them all and never get wide.

I'm not so lucky now, I guess.
Where I once said *More,* I now say *Less.*
Now I'm stuck with cottage cheese—
Don't show me pie, I beg you, please.

I know I'm not the only one
Who worries that I'll weigh a ton.
I weigh myself on Fridays too
So I can keep track, just like you.

Don't ever change this part of your show;
The reason is clear, I want you to know.
Without this weight check, I would be
Heavier yet by another fifty!"
—*Unsigned,* Bristol, Ct.

"Imagine? Somebody just drank the last cuppa coffee and didn't make a fresh pot!"

"Now tell me again... which button do I push..."

The Goose that Laid
the Golden Egg
or Bob's Recipe For Success

How does a person survive the changes which occur in any job over half a century? More than in other media, radio reflects changes in society: the big band sound becomes acid rock, and the mellow, soft-spoken announcer becomes the wild and crazy broadcaster with his own distinctive style.

Radio announcers have to fine-tune their formats and "airwave personalities" so that listeners will continue to tune in their program, and not another's. Advertisers, aware of the tremendous market a good announcer reaches, constantly scout the airwaves for the right person to sell their products.

Much more than just a science, advertising is also big business. Since the advent of television, radio has had to compete more effectively for its audience. To keep its advertisers, radio has had to keep its listeners. The announcer is the key. How has Bob Steele ridden the pendulum of changing times so successfully?

"I have been a loyal and appreciative listener to Bob Steele for more than 30 years. Over that period . . . I have marvelled at the broad and continuing appeal of Bob's character and personality, and his ability to survive the drastic changes in taste reflected in the musical context in which he has had to function these last years.
Bob's personality as a rugged American individualist, dedicated to solid middle class values, shines through to his listeners as a beacon light in the darkness of value-neutrality and moral relativism, even though he never

directly lectures or preaches. He offers . . . something dependable and unchanging to hold on to in order not to be swept away by overwhelming currents of change.

But, he is also one of the most effective, natural and persuasive salesmen the radio industry ever produced. When he is presenting a quality product or service in which he believes, his conviction and persuasion are remarkably effective."
—*John Schramm*, Redding, Ct.

Folksy Bob, with his daily dose of important trivia, holds the nation's number one share of audience listeners. He has had as much as 40% of the listening audience in the greater Hartford area, and his tremendous appeal helps account for WTIC's ever-growing popularity.

> **"**Hurray for you again! When I started to read about WTIC on page six of the *Hartford Courant,* I said to myself, 'When are they going to get to Bob Steele, the man who makes it all happen?' Then, they did—a whopping 35.9% share of the audience! And so well deserved! I feel proud! . . . It couldn't happen to a better man. Kudos to you!"—*Lillian Custer*

Everybody knows how Bob's done it—but each offers a differing opinion. The thread common to them all is that Bob has what it takes to get them up and get them going. He seems to understand that in that hectic hour after sleep and before work, we operate on half-charged batteries. Always running late, we forget to do the things that we need to do like mailing letters, bringing our lunch, or remembering the car keys. He also reminds us of the infrequent but important responsibilities we all face, like renewing our automobile licenses, calling Aunt Sadie on her birthday, and arranging for Fido to see the vet. His voice gently cuts through the blur of sleepiness like our parents' did way back when, reminding us to sit up straight . . . "doesn't that feel better?" Single handedly, he gets each one of us, a goodly portion of Connecticut, going for the day.

> **"**Thanks so much for the reminder when you said, 'Have you checked your drivers' license expiration date?' I thought that no one could possibly forget to renew their license. But on a whim, I checked mine, and I couldn't believe that it had

expired. I had to spend most of the next morning at the Motor Vehicle Department, but it was worth it. Thanks again for the reminder."–*Nancy Lee*, Hartford, Ct.

It isn't only what Bob tells you, it's how he tells you. Linking the important and the necessary, are the trivial and the ordinary, that more than 200,000 of us have come to listen for each day. Even the most sophisticated among us enjoys Uncle Bent, the "little things of little importance" from the news, and knowing the temperature in Saskatchewan. You learn more from Bob than you think you do.

Helpful hints from Bob:

> *For windows that sparkle, try a cleaning solution of ½ cup*
> *of ammonia, ½ cup of white vinegar and two tablespoons*
> *of cornstarch to a bucket of warm water.*

> *To restore the new look to patent-leather shoes and bags,*
> *apply a cloth moistened with white vinegar and then wipe*
> *down with a clean cloth.*

Who else would bother to recognize that some of us have trouble keeping our shoelaces tied tight enough? Who among us would admit to that fact? But Bob just knows, and then sets out to help us out—so we have one thing less to worry about in the morning.

"One morning months ago, I heard you telling us how to tie our shoes so that they would stay tied. I tried then to do it exactly that way and saw that it was a double knot to begin with and I know that that is a secure way to begin with. I knew I was not doing the rest right, and by experimenting a little, I found that I had to reverse from the way I had always done it before. It now stays tied!
The reason I am writing to you now, is because that whole procedure is so very vital to me! I am recovering from a foot operation and . . . I am using a walker. I have to hop on my left foot which has my 'top sider' shoe on it so I won't slip. By my tying the ties right I don't have to bend down to retie them all the time—thanks to you!"—*Bernice Smith*, Wilbraham, Mass.

"Now that you have taught us to tie our shoelaces so that they won't untie, could you please do me a favor and tell us how to *untie* them. I tried the tying technique on my jogging shoes last week, and found they really stayed laced! However, I'm getting married next Saturday, and feel that sneakers will not go too well with my tux . . ."—*Tony Michaelson*

Bob is a man who has a way of talking to almost one quarter of a million people as if each of them was the only one listening. He seems to know exactly what is going on in your life at that crazy hour of the morning, and it doesn't seem to surprise him one bit. Because he is ordinary folk like ourselves, he seems to have a magical sixth sense about what goes on in our homes. For instance, as a family man who raised four children, he has a very clear perception of kids at the breakfast table. For decades, he has managed to convince the children of Connecticut that this "man of Steele" had x-ray vision, long before any of their "superheroes" did.

" About twenty years ago, my daughter Judy spilled her orange juice at the breakfast table. Before she or I could react, your voice came over the radio, saying, 'I see a little girl who just spilled her juice.' Well, you could have knocked us both over. Your timing was perfect—and for the longest time, Judy believed that you had magic powers."—*Josephine D. Mascolo*, West Hartford, Ct.

" I was helping my (kindergarten-age) son get ready for school. He was buttoning up his shirt, and you said right at that time, 'Boy, that's a snappy shirt you've got on.' And he said, 'Ma, how can Bob Steele see my shirt?'"—*Mrs. Raymond Pace*, Torrington, Ct.

" When in school, I think I was in the second grade, one morning you were saying '. . . and there's some young fellow out there drinking his orange juice. You can't beat a nice fresh glass of that stuff.' Of course, I was one of probably a

thousand kids downing orange juice and listening at that instant, but I was so impressed. I had to tell the teacher about it that morning."—*Al Blank*, Bristol, Ct.

" Thirty years ago, my son John, who was eight years old, was having his breakfast. I looked out of the window, and saw his large pet duck fly over the fence. When I told him, he dashed out of the front door . . . and ran all the way up the street, crossed a lot, and ran into the Woodland School yard where he retrieved his pet.
When he came in the house to finish his breakfast, he heard Bob Steele say (on the radio, of course) to the school children, 'Did you empty the waste baskets yet? You must do it before you leave for school.'
John stopped eating and said, 'What a guy. What's so hard about emptying a waste basket? Didn't he see what I had to do to catch my dumb duck?' "—*Mrs. C. Wilkas*, Manchester, Ct.

Although we grown-ups like to think we're a lot more sophisticated than our youngsters, we all have a little bit of the innocent kid in us. Of course, we know that Bob really can't see us, but just try to convince us that this is so!

" At 6:15 one morning several years ago, when I should have been up and around, I was fast sinking into a much needed slumber, when I was very quickly awakened after you had on Frank Sinatra's record of *Nancy With The Laughing Face* . . . and . . . you admonished me in what I considered a truly solicitous and earnest manner, 'Nancy, are you awake?' In my somnolent state, I truly believed you were addressing me personally. Anyway, I did jump right out from between the soft, warm sheets and managed to make it to the old place of business on time."—*Nancy Newsom*, Old Saybrook, Ct.

You say you can see me, tuning in.
How great is my shame and my chagrin.
I have not yet applied my public face—
My private one is truly a disgrace.

My nose a-shine between half-opened eyes;
(For morning beauty I'll never take a prize).
My upper bridge still in a glass doth rest.
My hair looks like an old bird's nest.

My faded pink robe with the buttons gone
Is what I always wear to greet the dawn.
From six to eight I go about
In frayed green slippers with my toes poking out.

I haven't yet bound up this droopy form
Into a better sample of the human norm.
Your X-ray vision I deplore:
Don't say, 'I see you there!' any more.

The diplomat thinks twice before saying nothing.

WHOA!
GREAT SCOTT— I FORGOT! IT'S SUNDAY!
BOB STEECE
-RLS
SCREECH!

"How can you see through the radio?... The radio doesn't seem to have to be on for you to know what I'm saying. More than once I've asked myself, 'What time is it,' turned on the radio, and the first words you say are, 'The time is...'" —*Susan Staneslow*, Cheshire, Ct.

"As my sister and I would be getting ready for school each morning in the forties, the radio was always on and you would be helping us on our way. We were positive that you had enchanted powers when you would say,'I can see you out there' or 'Sit up straight.' You always caught me slumping. How did you do that, Bob?"—*Patricia Zawacki*, Meriden, Ct.

A man with vision always gets ahead of a man with visions.

Bob is like a member of the family across the breakfast table, or a good friend in the carpool. He knows just how you feel about running late, those extra pounds, the icy going and that tough Whaler's loss. Maybe that's why we appreciate his corny jokes.

"You are wonderful company for me every day on my way to work... I hate to drive on icy roads, and it is great to have such a reassuring friend in the car with me...."—*Joan Billings*, Stamford, Ct.

You heard about the duck that went into the drug store for some chopsticks. The clerk said, "Will this be cash or charge?" The duck said, "Put it on my bill."

"I heard your story about the driver who was stopped at the red light when the woman behind him 'honked' her horn because his sign on his car said to. The driver got out of his car and yelled at her because she *did* honk. That's the kind of thing I needed to hear to get me going this morning. I laughed all the way down Asylum Street to the office. Thanks for the cheer."—*P.R.T.*, Avon, Ct.

But don't be fooled by his mild mannered delivery. Bob Steele is a professional. His greatest asset is that for fifty years, rain, hail or snow, sickness or health, he has always been there. (The one exception to this rule is his annual Florida vacation.) He is the essence of dependability, stability, and tranquility. In this state of steady habits, Bob is the symbol of consistency that personifies New Englanders. There is a quality about this man that inspires trust. He is believable.

> "He is sentimental. He is always interested. He is someone you know who is wise, dependable, nobody's fool. You wish he lived next door."—*James Playsted Wood,* This Is Advertising, Crown Publishers, Inc. 1968 pg. 114

> "Bob is a living legend, and a consummate professional. He truly is a phenomenon in this business. His credibility level is unprecedented..."—*Tom Barsanti,* The Ten Eighty Corporation/WTIC AM-FM

When Bob says it's 9:30, it is. When he tells you it's minus 10 degrees in Calgary, you know it's no warmer. And if he tells you to try a product because you'll like it, you probably will. The reason is that Bob has tried it too.

Although he doesn't have final say over what WTIC advertises on his show, he is consulted and his opinions are valued. He will not say something is good unless he knows it to be so. For instance, he will not advertise ladies intimate apparel because he obviously has no first hand knowledge of this. But, if he has had a bad experience with a product, or hears complaints, he is quick to alert station executives so that they can re-evaluate the claims of the advertiser. Consistency and believability make Bob Connecticut's most sought after advertiser.

> "You are an excellent advertiser, and when you tell about a product or service, it is told lucidly and with that attention to detail which is sometimes lacking in much advertising today.
> I begin my day with you and your example gives me the courage to get out of bed and get motivated for whatever comes along."—*Howard Burdick,* Westerly, R.I.

> "Bob sent me this cartoon one Christmas and I thought it was really great—got a good chuckle out of it....! His style makes him a great advertiser."—*Peter L. Brown,* Peter L. Brown Siding Co.

" You and I have been together a long time. Congratulations on your 50th anniversary on WTIC. We're celebrating our 100th this year . . . hope you'll be around another 100 years for us."–*Al Guida,* Guida-Seibert Dairy

Doing business without advertising is like winking in the dark. You know what you are doing, but nobody else does.

Listeners often compare Bob's radio personality to that of the late Arthur Godfrey. But, Bob feels that his style is his own. Actually, he seems to have been more influenced by Paul Douglas, who used to announce baseball scores on the Chesterfield show with Fred Waring in the 1930s. Bob always liked the comfortable feeling of listening to Paul; his low-key, soft-spoken voice, gentle but so rich and smooth. Like Godfrey and Douglas, Bob is a mellow man with an-easy-to-listen to style.

" The late Arthur Godfrey (God rest his soul) always said only one person at a time listened to him—if there were others in the room, no one listened, so he always talked to just one person, easily and quietly. You seem to do the same, and that's the way I like it!"–*Marion Conant*

As professional a broadcaster as Bob is, it is fitting to end with some thoughts about his special brand of humor, for after all, it is humor that is the key to his success.

Although he appreciates the zany comedy of Henny Youngman, Sid Caesar and Red Skelton, Bob's laid back humor is much more subtle, in the style of Bob Newhart and Don Adams, two comedians he greatly admires. He delights in delivering a not-so-funny line, or perhaps a small play on words, with just the right touch, and you both share a chuckle. He has an appreciation for the ridiculous.

Bob often finds the ridiculous in the ordinary. While most of his jokes come from things he's heard or read, they often originate from out of the blue, triggered by who knows what.

One day, while on line at the bank, Bob observed a fastidious janitor emptying the trash, and assumed that "he must be the Head Trashier."

He scans the teletypes, papers, and magazines for the tidbit that tickles his fancy. He assumes that you'll love it too. His listeners are his partners in crime; they too cull their own sources for jokes that they know he'll enjoy. Sometimes, to their delight, Bob will read their contribution on the air so the rest of us can join in the giggling, too.

It is this communication of humor that has made Bob Steele so successful for so long. Thank you, Dear Bob.

Early in the misty morn,
As I wake to greet the dawn,
Your voice, ever calm and mellow
Reminds me you're my a.m. fellow.

My day's begun, I'm on my way
To do what I have to do that day.
It's scrambled eggs à la Steele
You know how great that makes me feel!

I comb my hair; I grab my case
I look around, and all's in place.
I go to turn the radio down
For in my car I'll still hear your sound.

Thanks for the tip, I forgot my lunch,
As for your prediction, you've got the wrong hunch.
I loved the one about the lady from Spain,
But your last joke was truly a pain!

I heard a great joke yesterday
For this, one dollar you will pay.
Dear Bob, you cheer me way down deep.
You're a special friend I'll always keep.

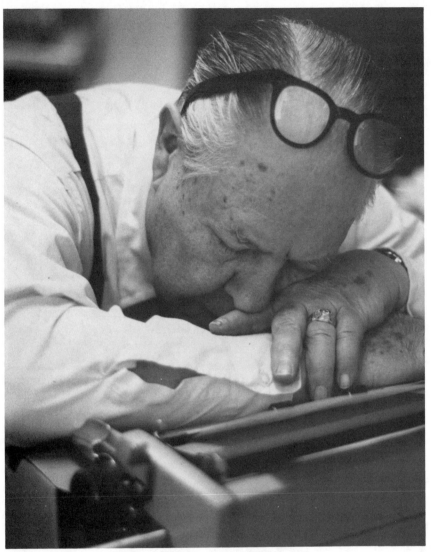

"Of course, sometimes take a quick snooze."

"We've just heard Bob and Ray, the funniest pair on this planet. I love 'em!"

Believe It Or Don't

One day a priest was our ringing the bell of his church. He was approached by a man who came and said, "Father, there is something I've been wanting to do for a long time." "What is that, my son?" asked the priest. "I've been wanting to ring those bells myself." "Well," said the kindly priest, "you may go ahead if you want to." The man backed up three feet and ran, hitting his face into the bell. "Boy, that was fun," said the man. "Can I do it again?" The priest was a bit surprised, but agreed. Again the man backed up, ran, and hit his face into the bell. "I don't really like watching you do this," said the priest, but the man begged and begged for another turn, and reluctantly the puzzled priest agreed. The man backed up, ran, but missed the bell, and fell over the balcony, and was dead. The priest hurried down to the street, and asked the gathering crowd if anyone knew the deceased man. One woman replied, "I don't know his name, but, boy, his face sure rings a bell!"

What's Turkey Day without turkey? Difficult.

    While other folks eat stuffed turkey, vegetarian Gretchen Greer of Grand Rapids, Michigan, will have stuffed pumpkin. She says that it has become her "Thanksgiving thing." It takes at least two days to prepare. Gretchen claims that stuffed Thanksgiving pumpkin requires as much work as the traditional turkey feast.

During the holiday season, it's a good idea to learn where to find the wise old birds of the turkey-cooking business.

Some are with Swift and Company in Chicago. For Thanksgiving, they set up a toll-free hotline for confused cooks who wanted to talk turkey. And, judging from the questions, there were plenty of people who really needed help.

A typical question: "Is it OK to thaw a turkey in the dryer?"
No.

❝You said that one day while you were driving your car, you came up behind a guy driving a panel truck on the highway. You noticed that every so often, the guy would swing a baseball bat out the window and whack the side of his truck with it. Finally, after seeing him do this many times, your curiosity got the best of you. You pulled up next to him at a stop light, and asked him what he was doing. He told you he had a two ton truck with three tons of canaries in it, and he had to keep at least one ton of canaries flying all the time so the truck wouldn't be overloaded."–*Harold T. Flaherty, Broad Brook, Ct.*

*Marlene Lambert said: "We figured TV was going to the dogs."
So, why not produce some TV that's strictly for the dogs? That's
the thinking behind a half-hour video-cassette she's produced
for Kartes Video, entitled "Arf!" The idea is that when humans
leave the house, Rover, who can be trained to work the TV set's
remote control, can amuse and educate himself by viewing the
video staion "WDOG." It offers such delightful segments as dog
news, dog sports, etc. All this is hosted by real life dogs who
speak in dog language. However, English language captions are
supplied for humans who want to join in the fun.*

**Ad in the paper: "Whosoever stole my fire extinguisher out of
my car—Where you are going, you will need it.!"**—*Walter L.*
Brown, East Hartford, Ct.

*He used to be Rex Robert Frink; then, one night he dreamed of
a name change. He decided to do just that. He went to a judge
in Austin, Minnesota, and told him he wanted to change his
name to one with a "literal meaning." The judge agreed, and
Rex Robert Frink is now Welcome Pleasure Freely. However, the
judge warned Freely, "Don't expect it to be easy to cash a check."*

*A man planning to become a doctor felt a name change was in
order, reports King County, Wash. Commissioner Maurice Ep-
stein. So now the future doctor is Thomas Edward Jirgensohn.
His last name was changed from "Kill." Meanwhle, in Penang,
Malaysia, people with colds know where to go—Ah Choo Medical
Hall. That's where Dr. Choo Ah Choo has his offices.*—L.A. Daily
News, *Herb Caen, San Francisco Chronicle*

> **We all know cruises can be great**
> **But I think it should be said**
> **That while they put you in the pink—**
> **They sure do leave you in the red!**

*There were more people running for national office in 1984
than Ronald Reagan and Walter Mondale. You could find the
following:*
> *Dodge, Ford, Bentley or Carr.*
> *Snow, Frost or Winter.*

Caesar and Nero. Mason and Dixon. Lewis and Clark.
Bell, Ringer. Hunter, Skinner.
Hill, Fields, Brooks, Grove, Boggs. Ridge and Stump.
Rockefeller and Dupont. Swank.
House, Hall and Castle.
England and Ireland.
Lotta, Bull.

"I went into Parson's Hardware store and asked—'Can I get some nails?' The clerk said, 'Sure. How long do you want them?' And I said—'To keep!'"—*Walt McGowan*

The burial of her 50-year-old daughter in a Vallejo, California cemetery caused Susie Martin "extreme disgust" and she filed a lawsuit in Oakland against Sunrise Memorial Cemetery. Martin claims that when the grave turned out to be too small for the casket, gravediggers wanted to turn it on its side until they were stopped by the distressed mourners. They tried to break off the

casket's ornate handles to get it to fit. At that point, she says, attendants actually began to jump up and down on the coffin to get it into the grave. When the lid caved in, they called it a day. The deceased was finally laid to rest some six days later.
—San Francisco Chronicle

Bell Hop: "Did I hear you ring, sir?" Irate Guest: "No, I was tolling. I was sure you were dead."

A lieutenant, newly commissioned and just out of OCS, was reviewing a group of men in Company "B" Battalion. He was very nervous, and had a great deal of difficulty getting the men's attention. The lieutenant, who was very short in stature, heard a voice at the back of the group say, "and a little child shall lead them." At this, there was laughter all around, and the formation broke up.

Later, the following notice was posted on the company bulletin board: "Co. 'B' will fall out at midnight for a 20 mile forced march with full packs—and a little child shall lead them—on a very big horse."

You know that your teenagers have finally grown up when they:
> *Leave the car with gas in it, and a note that they've checked the oil and tires.*
> *Put their money into the bank instead of into record albums.*
> *Ask for your advice and are impressed with how much you know.*
> *Sit with their feet on the floor instead of hanging them over the arm of the chair.*
> *Get a haircut before you start threatening to braid it.*
> *Are in possession of a postage stamp that you can borrow.*
> *Tell you that they've used the last of the peanut butter.*

Little boy to his dog: "Mom says I can't take a cookie without asking first. Can I have permission to have a cookie, Spot?"

> "My Uncle Jack had just bought new skin diving gear, and he wanted to try it out. He went to the beach, and put everything on, and then he went in twenty feet. Another man went in twenty feet without any gear on, so my Uncle Jack said to himself, 'I'll show him.' He went in forty feet, but so

did the man without any gear. My Uncle took out his writing tablet, and wrote: *Why are you out 40 feet without any gear on?* The man grabbed the tablet, and wrote back: *You idiot! I'm drowning!—Maria Forti, Enfield, Ct.*

Donald Johansen, supervisor of secondary education, Minnesota Department of Education, says it used to be relatively easy to spot the principal of a school. It was always the person with a master's degree and two losing seasons. Things are not so simple now, and Johansen offers the following checklist to help spot the principal of a school. He claims that this list will identify the principal 98% of the time.

The principal is the one who has a back with a funny kink in it and a blood pressure of 170/90, yet doesn't hesitate to carry in extra chairs at any public meeting.

The principal is the one who holds three University degrees, yet regularly spends a substantial percentage of time each day inspecting lavatories.

The principal is the one whose nose is corroded from locker rooms, chemistry experiments, paint sprays, and burned food, but can pick out a tiny whiff of marijuana smoke in a football crowd of 2,000.

The principal is the one who rages like a wild animal while discussing attendance with a truant student, yet sheds a tear when the homecoming queen says "thank you" to mom and dad, teachers and friends.

The principal is the one whose will to live was lost two weeks before Spring break yet beams with honest pride at graduation when each diploma is issued.

Soccer fans of Nigeria's "Ibadan Shooting Stars" team are itching for revenge, after an African Cup game in Togo. Apparently, fans of the rival "Semassi Sokoda" team showered them with itching powder, which left them scratching for days after the game. Fortunately, it was the team from Togo who took a powder, losing 6-3.—London Times

A couple was watching a baseball game in Fenway Park. The husband was trying to explain the complexities of the game

to his wife. "Look," he cried excitedly. "We've got a man on every base!" "But dear," replied his wife, "so has the other team."

They arrived during the 5th inning of the game. "What is the score?" she asked her date. "Nothing to nothing," he replied. "Oh, goodie. Aren't we lucky?" she exclaimed. "We haven't missed anything."

How to Recognize a Company Car

> Company cars travel faster in all gears, especially reverse.
> They accelerate at a phenomenal rate.
> They enjoy a much shorter braking distance.
> They have a much tighter turning radius.
> They can take bumps at twice the speed of private cars.
> Oil and tire pressures, battery and water levels don't need to be checked nearly so often.
> The floor is shaped like an ashtray.
> They don't have to be garaged at night.
> They need cleaning less often, especially the interior.
> The tire walls are designed to permit bumping into and over curbstones.
> No security is needed. The cars may be left anywhere, unlocked and with the keys in the ignition.
> Unusual and alarming engine noises are easily eliminated by listening to the Bob Steele Show on WTIC-1080 and turning up the volume. Turn it *way* up!

My Grandma is a with it old lady. She always wears roller skates while she sits in her rocking chair. She says she does it so she can rock and roll!

A father who owned several Midwestern newspapers brought his son into the business. After many years, and having worked his way up to only a minor executive position, the son suggested that the company would benefit from a mandatory retirement age of 65. The father agreed, although ruled that it would apply to everyone except himself. Through his 50s, 60s and 70s the father continued daily to come to the office. Finally, when the

father was 97 years young and still running the company, he called his son in, and informed him: "Son, you're now 65. You've got to retire—it's company policy."

Notice on the Company Bulletin Board:

Due to increased competition and a keen desire to remain in business, we find it necessary to institute a new policy, effective immediately.

We are asking that somewhere between starting and quitting time, and without infringing too much on the time usually devoted to lunch period, story telling, coffee breaks, rest periods, ticket selling, the rehashing of yesterday's TV programs, and discussion of engagement rings, that each employee try to find some time that can be set aside. This will be known as the "work break."

Some undoubtedly will see this as a radical innovation, but we honestly believe the idea has great possibilities. It may even be an aid to steady employment; it might be a means of assuring steady paychecks. While the adoption of the "work break" plan is not compulsory, we trust that each employee will find the time to try it out.

"I hear on the radio," said one Russian to another, "that we are producing large quantities of meat, butter and milk. But still my refrigerator is always empty. What should I do?" Suggested the other Russian: "Plug your refrigerator directly into your radio."

A lot of modern music is improved by bad reception on radio.

Linda Coffee spends eight hours a day in the kitchen of her Minneapolis home baking snacks for the dogs. Judging by the aroma escaping from her oven, humans would find them pretty appealing too. But you see, these are true gourmet treats, which she sells under the brand name of "Haute Canine." She uses all natural ingredients, and sells them to stores like Bloomingdale's and Saks Fifth Avenue. The cost to the consumer? $7.50 for a 10 ounce bag.

" The Chief had three wives, one of whom lived in a tepee made of deer hide, and she had two sons. The second wife lived in a tepee made of elk hide, and also had two sons. The third wife lived in a tepee of hippopotamus hide, and had four sons. From this information, it's easy to see that the sons of the squaw of the hippopotamus equals the sons of the squaws of the other two hides.—*Dennie Lunt*, Greenfield, Mass.

Helpful Household Hints from Uncle Bob:

If you want to protect woolens from moths without using moth balls, and you don't have a cedar closet, try this trick. Use cedar chips or strips, which can be found in your local lumber yard. Put them in nylon net bags, line a large drawer with the strips, or just sprinkle them in the drawers where you are storing your woolens. Be sure to cover the cedar with tissue, and you're on your way to good smelling, moth-proof protection.

Activated charcoal is a great mildew deterrent. Not only will a few pieces of charcoal strategically placed in a closet absorb moisture, but it will absorb odors as well. Although you must be sure to replace the charcoal every so often, the result is well worth the time and effort.

What did William Tell say to his boy as he placed an apple on his head? "I'm going to miss you, Son."

A 98 year old beekeeper says he gets a real buzz out of being stung. "I love stings," he says. "It seems to liven you up." That happens at least six times a week at his home in Red Bay, Ontario (Canada). And he isn't the only beekeeper who swears by the healthful benefits of stings. In fact, the Canadian Bee-keepers Association has set up a fund to finance research into the effects of bee venom on arthritis and rheumatism. That's encouraging news for sufferers of those ailments. Let's hope they'll come up with another way to inject it.—Canadian Press

A teacher asked her class to tell her what plant reminded them of Easter if the poinsettia plant reminded them of Christmas. A little girl eagerly replied: "An egg plant."

Bob's Connecticut Trivia:

The State Capitol in Hartford was designed by the 19th century architect Richard M. Upjohn. It is made of white marble, and has a gilded dome.

The Connecticut River is the largest river in New England.

All literate citizens, at least 21 years of age, who are not convicts and have resided in the State one year and in the town six months, may register to vote.

Connecticut has eight votes in the Electoral College.

Connecticut ranks as the 48th state in land area with 5,009 square miles.

The Connecticut motto is *Qui Transtulit Sustinet* (He Who Transplanted Sustains).

The Connecticut tree is the white oak, the state flower is the mountain laurel, and the bird, the American robin.

"Great town, Hartford. I'm glad they let me stay."

Robert L. (for Elmer) Steele

"Bob Steele.

The name conjures up memories of a prediction that the St. Louis Browns would win the pennant . . .

That a certain lion in a British zoo could be counted on to make a little boy his dinner every year . . .

That Milt Famey would lose the World Series, also every year . . .

That Bob's show would be the only reliable source of information about all the good Connecticut folks who reached their 80th birthday or more . . .

That the word for the day would invariably be one I had been mispronouncing all my life . . . and . . . .

That, if I really wanted to know the temperature in Caribou, Maine, the only place I could find it would be on Bob Steele's program. . . .

It is a tribute to Bob that, in spite of getting out of bed at an unheard of hour of the day to entertain and inform the people of Connecticut six mornings a week, he has still found the time to be involved in a host of civic, community and charitable activities which have benefited so many throughout Connecticut.

I am sure I speak for the vast majority of the citizens of our state when I wish Bob well on his 50th anniversary on WTIC, and to tell him that he will be welcome in our homes for many more years."–*The Honorable William A. O'Neill,* Governor, State of Connecticut

"I have had the pleasure of meeting Bob on several occasions. I listen to his program whenever I can. I marvel at his continuing appeal. . . . He is a genuinely kind and compassionate, family-oriented person who represents traditional values. He reminds us that there is yet stability in our environment. To listen to him is to return to where we are secure. . . . For New England, the 'Land of Steady Habits,' he is always there. . . . Like Arthur Godfrey, he is a man whom we can trust."—*John DiBiaggio,* former President, University of Connecticut

The Citizen of the Week chosen by Station WRCH during the first week in November, 1966, was a formidable WRCH competitor named Robert L. Steele. WRCH had this to say about Bob:

"Robert Lee Steele—former boxer, Hollywood extra, sports prognosticator of dubious distinction, teller of tall tales, breakfast bon vivant and *the* most talked-about broadcasting personality in Connecticut during the past 30 years. Rich Music is proud to salute this fellow broadcaster,

known to thousands throughout Southern New England as 'your good friend and mine'. . . Bob Steele. This month Bob has celebrated his 30th year with WTIC; he observed 24 years as the most listened-to morning personality last May. Robust Robert has preeminently qualified himself for consideration as Citizen of the Week because of the multitude of good cheer he has brought to shut-ins, our senior citizens, our growing youngsters and morning commuters. Three generations of radio listeners have come to rely on him as they would a member of the family. Bob Steele ranks with Don McNeil, Arthur Godfrey and Art Linkletter as one of the most able communicators in the country. As a husband, as a father, as a man, Bob Steele has been a credit. WRCH is indeed gratified to acknowledge this most worthy competitor, for in doing so, we acknowledge our own Broadcasting Industry as a responsible industry . . ."

"You sent me off to school, and you sent our children to school or announced those glorious no school days. The children have grown, left home and you are still helping my husband and me move through the morning routine.
You are a happy, positive, uplifting way to start the day. You have kept high standards. You have given pleasure, good advice, and kept us on schedule.
For all this and more, I say thank you."—*Ann T. Hall*, Agawam, Mass.

"When I was ten years old and entering a new school, I became very nervous on the first day of school. So, my mom said, 'Listen to Bob Steele and his voice will calm your nerves.' So I did! I listened to your jokes, your Children's Hour, and your calming voice for 25 years.
Now, as fate would have it, I became a teacher. I still get nervous the first day of school, but I want you to know it's very comforting to be able to switch you on.
Thank you for being there!"—*Diane K. Deggan*, South Windsor, Ct.

"I may become a night person!
Every morning since I can remember I have started my day with Bob Steele. Years back I had breakfast with him,

dressed my children and got them ready and off to school with him. I kept up with the outside world through him and had my first laugh of the day with him. I even cleaned my house as he whistled along with good music.

Now my children are grown and gone, but I still have breakfast and the first laugh of the day with Bob. Now I get myself dressed and off to school; Bob drives in with me. We still enjoy the same kind of music. I really can't imagine starting the day without him.

So, when he retires, I guess I'll just sleep in and become a night person. What an awful thought!"—Another whistler, *Ginny Francois*, Storrs, Ct.

"When I was a 'little girl,' I anxiously awaited your children's story. Obediently, I 'cleaned my plate,' and 'drank my milk.' (Was it 'chug-a-lug'?) Through the years, you became our morning guest, friend and bearer of the joyous snow cancellations to school.

Five years ago, I returned to West Hartford, and was so

happy to hear you, again, every morning. Now, my teenager delights in your orderly school cancellations! Perhaps you represent security in those memories of family . . . and youth. More pertinent, you have become 'a friend.' To paraphrase a slogan, 'Coffee without Bob Steele is like a day without sunshine.'"—*Sue Stramm*, West Hartford, Ct.

"I've been listening to you for years and years. (I can't remember when you were not the first voice I heard in the morning.)

When I was teaching school back in the '60s, I used your 'daily word' as my 'daily word' and increased the vocabulary of my students.

Many times—but many!—you reminded me to take my letters to be mailed; to take my dinner out of the freezer.

I sympathized with you when you were trying to lose weight (how many times?) and listened to the daily ounces you lost.

I remember your jokes, but the one I remember most vividly is the one about a woman's brain. One morning you said, 'You know a woman's brain is divided in two parts . . . (long pause) . . . Dollars and Cents!' I didn't know whether to laugh or get mad at you. I still have not decided, but I do chuckle every time I think of it.

I'm really glad to share moments of my life with you. You are like an 'old friend.' "—*Edith Prague*, Representative, Eighth District

"Hearing your familiar voice on radio often makes me feel thankful for one stable and familiar four-hour period (4½) in this hectic world. . . . After listening for all these many years (about 22, I think), I am thankful for Bob Steele. You calm my nerves, and tickle my 'funny bone,' as I'm sure you do and have done for many others!

P.S. You have the best voice I ever heard."—*Lillian Custer*, Manchester, Ct.

"On behalf of the Actuaries' Club of Hartford and myself, I'd like to thank you for a job well done. You are truly the most enjoyable and entertaining speaker the Club has had in its history."—*Michael Braunstein*, President, Actuaries' Club of Hartford

"We have been listening to you since you started on the 6:30 p.m. sports news, and have continued since then, but never gave you a few words of applause as encouragement to continue, which you do deserve from all your listeners. I finally realized that to you, it must seem at times you are 'talking to the wall'...

Over the years, from your program at different intervals, we knew when it was time to start the morning coffee, when to awaken the children for school and later on, when to go to work, and other helpful things to us.

I realized how our son had become an adult when he said he now listens to the Bob Steele program on his way to work with his car pool, when he used to listen to 'rock music' as a teenager.

We wish you Good health, a Long Life, and hope you continue bringing happiness to many households, like part of the morning sunshine."—*Max Seger,* Colchester, Ct.

"I am writing this letter on behalf of my mother, *Margaret Oris*...

She would have written this letter herself, but she is unable to do so since she has been in a state of trauma since your latest (and this is *not* the *first*) tardiness for your program on WTIC.

She has been a regular listener since the 1930s, on various G.E. and Philco radio models, and now listens to you on a tiny transistor model. In spite of the fluctuations of radio-receiver technology, she has been an ever-faithful listener. *However,* your second tardiness in the past forty years has led her to the following conclusions:

You fly-by-night kids who want to break into show business and make it big on radio had better learn about punctuality! If you expect to have *any* kind of career in radio, you'd just better get your act together, Buster, and get to the studio on time!

She is, however, compassionate, and willing to give you another chance. If you promise not to be late again, she'll keep her little transistor tuned to you.

P.S. I've been in Michigan since 1966, but still have the

fondest memories of listening to Bob Steele for a-l-l of those mornings so many, many years ago . . . As a very little boy I heard your morning program before I ran to catch the bus; as a middle-aged man I'm writing you light-heartedly on behalf of my mother. I suspect the compliment needs no further adornment."–*Bob Oris*, Dearborn Heights, Michigan

"Want you to know that the Blood Mobile in Avon did very well on Monday October 10th, due to WTIC making folks aware of the program. Amazing how many folks came in saying they heard Bob Steele's plea for help. So you see, Bob, your good work does pay off!"–*Ann M. Radin*, Avon, Ct.

"I have been one of your many fans since I moved to Connecticut years ago. It is my opinion that the most wonderful gift you give to another is the gift of laughter. This gift you give to me every morning. You are one of the few people who can make me laugh at 5:45 a.m. I particularly like it when you read the list of names of people who have helped to make your show possible. By the end of the list, I am reduced to helpless giggling."–*Joan Nagy*, Tariffville, Ct.

"In 1946, my sisters and I purchased a small radio from your friend, Bill Savitt. We had a little payment card, where each installment was deducted. We had just gone on our own, had a furnished apartment and our new radio.
You became as much a member of our family as any relative. You were there . . . the day I got married. Your advice that morning was '. . . don't go out unless it's absolutely necessary.' Well, we had a blizzard that day with 15 degrees below zero. But Bill and I were married in Middletown. Our honeymoon was delayed as we could go no further than Hartford because of the snow. Now, 37 years later, I'm glad I didn't heed your advice.
You have been with us even when I was in the hospital becoming a mother four times. It was always comforting to have your voice chatting as though you were right there. Thank you for being a silent friend!
My sister still has the small old radio although we listen to you now on digital clock radios . . ."–*Carol Mann*, Middletown, Ct.

"You give my day a positive beginning, be it a giggle, a smile, or one of your great bad jokes. At a period of time when there is so much negativity, you always come through with fresh air and sunshine.

My all time favorite thing you do is to recite the poem of Wallace and the Ramsbottoms."–*Marcia Allard,* Terryville, Ct.

"Listening to your voice for so long, you've become, intangibly though it may be, a part of the fabric of our lives. . .

Your program was always a good way to start the morning. There seemed to be a relaxed quality about it, and a basic integrity that one learned to depend on; it was always easy-going, informative, unpretentious, never offensive, laced with crackling dry humor and subtle wit that sneaked up on you after a while. In short, it was easy to take . . . Just the other morning in a restaurant, I heard someone say: 'If Bob Steele said it, it's true.' I'm sure there is some kind of message there."–*Stanley Dabkowski,* New Britain, Ct.

"While sending this request for a copy of the recipe for 'Crabless Crab Salad,' I want to thank you for helping me keep my sanity and perspective over the years—with your unfailing good humor and contagious enjoyment of all of life's pleasures and goodness."–*Alice Curtis,* Bethlehem, Ct.

"Visited a Board Member in Newington yesterday, and she gave me the delightful news that she's pretty sure you announced our PSA regarding the importance of spaying cats now, before late-winter mating season results in thousands of kittens, born to die. She said you put it into your own words, which is absolutely great. Sorry I didn't hear it. . . . Thanks, Bob. You are a doll."–*Mildred Lucas,* President, The Foundation for Animal Protection, Inc., Brookfield Center, Ct.

"We saw your name mentioned in a 'Dear Abby' column in the Bangor Daily News last week, and it reminded us of what we missed most when we left Connecticut thirteen years ago . . . your radio program! We lived in East Hartford for 14 years, and really enjoyed your morning show.

You started our days off with a chuckle at a good joke or a groan at the corny stuff. Either way, you were a day brightener. Thank you for the many mornings we spent with you."–*John and Rosemary Hede*, Stockholm, Me.

"On behalf of the Winsted Chapter, I would like to thank you for your daily reminders last week that ours was to be the only Red Cross Bloodmobile in the state on Memorial Day. As a result, we collected 192 pints of blood. Of those donors, 70 were walk-ins, and 34 new first-time donors. And this is what keeps the Red Cross blood program going."–*Doris B. St.Onge*, American Red Cross, Winsted, Ct. Chapter

"I was one of the many who heard you speak today at the Torrington High School, and I just had to write to you and tell you how much I enjoyed your talk.
I was the one on your right who was hysterically laughing long before you reached the punch lines of most of your jokes, simply because I heard most of them on your morning radio show. . . .
When I, and most of my friends left, we were saying to ourselves (and each other for that matter): 'What *did* he say?' You didn't have to say anything. You brightened up everyone's day, and we all will be talking about this humanities program for a long while."–*Patrick S. Matrascia*, Torrington, Ct.

"Bob Steele's morning program was as traditional as 'apple pie.' He entertained and informed us on our way to school. His compassion for the young and the elderly was heart-warming, mentioning birthdays or deeds.
Even though his voice was convincing, many times he was just telling an anecdote. You got addicted to his program. At times you felt he was giving you fatherly advice . . .
I can't imagine the next 50 years without Bob on the air."–*Anne Mahalawich*, Association of Retired Teachers of Connecticut, Norwich, Ct.

"I have been a dedicated listener, despite threats of bodily harm from my mother, my room-mates, and now my wife, for the past thirty-six years. I first became addicted when *you* used to give me days off from first grade. The highlight of my educational process. I also remember rearranging my schedule as an adult to accommodate such stories as 'The Emperor's New Clothes' and 'Peter and the Wolf.'

However, the thing I remember most is when one Christmas season you offered 'Bob Steele On Record.' You assured your listeners that the studio was filled with several million of these records. I decided to be a nice guy, avoid the holiday confusion, wait 'till after the rush, etc., and order later. The day I had my order in hand you announced that your vast supply had been exhausted. You did say, however, that some might be returned. These would be sorted, rewrapped, and offered for sale later. Is now later? I would still like to purchase one of the records. . . ."—*Paul Elwell*, V.M.D., Roxbury, Ct.

" I hope you won't take offense to my calling you 'Bob,' for I do so out of a tremendous warmth that I feel whenever I hear your voice on my car radio while driving around up here in Amherst, Mass. where we live.

The first time that I happened by chance to be tuned to WTIC and hear you, it sent me hurtling back a hefty thirty-one years to dark winter mornings in Southwick, Mass. I was six years old then, coming sleepy-eyed to the breakfast table before school. The smell of toast and coffee filled the warm air, the sound of spoons and knives clinking on china plates, and your mellow voice on the radio dispensing newsy tidbits. I never stopped to focus on that scene, or those perceptions, then, because it was the same, with small variations, day after day—the smell, the warmth, your voice, the clinking of silverware, and I was just a child busy with the business of growing up. . . .

And so to look back at my childhood, when it seems sometimes so far away, if I want to recapture that wonderful early morning scene with the voluptuous smell of warm toast and the feeling of safety, 'All's right with the world,' all I have to do is tune in 1080 in the morning . . . and your resonant, mellow, comforting voice brings it all back, crystal clear. It just seems a sort of minor miracle to me that you are still there in that same place with that steady, mellow voice. Thank you for being part of my childhood and now my adulthood."—*Melanie Fletcher-Howell*

"Politicians, reporters and show people come and go, but Bob Steele continues as one of the finest morning radio personalities in America. He knows New Englanders, he knows his listeners, and he talks about what is important to them. Nobody does it better than Bob Steele. One half century of acclaimed broadcasting on the most powerful station in Connecticut speaks well for itself."—*Honorable Lowell P. Weicker, Jr.* United States Senator, Connecticut

"Well, that's another one down the chute. Let's try it again tomorrow.

Afterword

In recent comments to a group gathered to pay tribute to his radio career, Bob responded without a script.

Because they were ad lib remarks, they capture, perhaps better than any miticulously crafted comments, the quality and the style of the man.

I'm just thankful to the Lord that I could be at the same job at the same station for so long. Everything has happened just right for me, it seems.

I don't know how many of you know this story—I've probably told it half a dozen times on the air, but some of you are too young to remember. I think I stopped telling this story about forty-seven years ago.

When I came to Hartford, I came to announce the motorcycle races on a public address system. That was my job. I was in Los Angeles at the time, with the WPA, which was a very fine organization that FDR dreamed up to keep people from starving to death. I was one of those who survived because of the Works Progress Administration. I was working as a time keeper in a carrot field. For some reason that always gets a laugh, a carrot field, but I was working in a carrot field. I was a time keeper. It was my job to go down the rows seeing if everybody was at work.

One day a guy came running across the field—this is a true story—and he had a telegram. I couldn't imagine anybody bringing a telegram to me in the middle of a carrot field. It said "Come to

Hartford as soon as you can. You've got a job, $30 a week." Well, I was making $94 a month at the time. It took me a couple of days to figure out how much that was per week. I figured $30 a week came to $130 a month. I was making $94 a month with the WPA so I wired Hartford that I'd be there right away.

I arrived here on the 10th of May, 1936, bumming most of the way. My ride let me off near the Corning Fountain in Bushnell Park, right near the railroad station. It was 2 o'clock in the morning and about 40 degrees. I didn't even have a top coat. We didn't wear them in California, and I was freezing. I had a couple of suitcases made out of genuine cardboard, and they were coming apart. I went to the YMCA with two dimes in my pocket. So help me, this is a true story. I had 20¢ in my pocket. I'm worth ten times that today. The guy said "Sure, Room 601. That'll be $1." He wrote my name down, he put the room down. I said "I've only got 20¢, but I'll have the 80¢ to give you tomorrow." He said, "Gee, wait a minute. Let me check that list again." Then he said, "Oh, oh, I made a little mistake. We're full up. We don't have any rooms."

I walked out of there with my two dimes and I went to the Garde Hotel. Some of you are old enough to remember the Garde Hotel which is no longer in existence. They gave me a room upstairs, on the very top story, for $1.50. Since I was in a hotel, I didn't have to pay in advance. The next morning I called the race promoter, George Lannom, the man who'd hired me. He came down to meet me before check out time and gave me a $5 bill. I paid my $1.50 and left.

That was the beginning of it. I did the motorcycle races, the public address work, at Bulkeley Stadium for the season. The stadium is no longer standing, but that's not my fault.

At the end of the racing season, I was getting a ride back to California with one of the motorcycle racers who lived on the West Coast. It was the last day of September and I had a day to kill and nothing to do. I had always wanted to be a radio announcer. I had done a little bit of motorcycle and auto racing description on a station in Los Angeles called KGFJ, but I wasn't a staff man. I knew nothing about radio work. I just knew enough to talk about the races. I'd always wanted to go into radio, but I had gone to WDRC at one time during the summer in '36 for an audition. They gave me some news to read. "We'll call you." The old story. So I gave it up. I said I'd never make it because I'd taken auditions before at several LA stations—small stations—and I never made it. So I gave up the idea. But I had this day to kill, and I was in downtown Hartford.

It was about 3 o'clock in the afternoon. I went to the Princess Theatre on State Street. That's no longer there either, of course. State Street is still there, but the theatre's no longer there. The girl in the cage said "If you wait about twenty minutes or so, you can get in at the beginning of it. There's a mystery on." Just my luck. She said "Come back in about twenty-five minutes and you'll see the beginning of the thing. Go in now and you'll ruin it." What a lucky day! How many cashiers would even say that today?

So I had that time to kill and I walked across that green there into the Travelers Building, which was on Central Row. So help me, I walked right in, went up the stairs, and asked the elevator operator for WTIC. All the elevators had operators in those days. You couldn't punch a button and go where you wanted to go, you had to have a little pull, you know, and you had to know the elevator operator to get off at the right floor, and then maybe the elevator would be up a few inches off the floor. He took me up to the 6th floor in the Grove Street Building. I went in and just said, "Do you need any announcers here?"

This was in 1936. You couldn't buy a job in those days. People were starving to death. It was the height of the depression. And Fred Wade, the chief announcer there, said "As a matter of fact, we're looking for an announcer. We just auditioned thirteen guys about an hour ago." He said, "We'll give you a shot at it if you want to go in." I went in and took an audition. They gave me some news to read and some musical programs to announce. They wanted to see if I knew anything about composers like Bach, Beethoven, and all those fellows. I'd never heard of them, but they gave me the sheet and I read them just the way they looked. I didn't know how to pronounce them. I had never gone to college.

I went in and I talked to the boss afterwards and he said, "Well, if we can get the midwestern accent out of your speech, we'll give you a six-month trial." He said, "You've got to be from the midwest." I found out he was from Illinois himself and he knew western and midwestern accents when he heard one. So he said, "Back here we say hog, for example. H-o-g is hog, it isn't hawg." This is an absolute true story. I never saw him face-to-face again until three or four years later. Anytime I'd notice him in the hall, we had a long corridor there, and his office was way at the end and we were all up at the other end; well, if I'd see him coming out of his office into the hall to go to the elevator, I'd duck out. I'd avoid him because I wanted to go through this six-month period without any contact with him.

Imagine, if I hadn't gone to that particular theatre or if that girl hadn't said "Why don't you wait twenty-five minutes?" I'd have gone into the show and come out. I'd have left the next day for California. I might have stopped in Topeka, Kansas or Lawton, Oklahoma or some place and got a job at a filling station and my life would have been different. As it was, I stayed here.

I married a West Hartford girl who worked in the Travelers. I saw her on the elevator one day when I was going up to the sixth floor. She worked on the 11th. I asked the elevator operator—that was the beauty of the elevator operators in those days. I asked the guy who that beautiful girl was and he told me her name and said she worked on the 11th floor.

I wrote her a note and asked her if she would consider a date. I said that I'm in WTIC and I figured that would be a big thing and she'd say, "Oh, boy." We had an engineer by the name of Al Jackson. Al had a 1930 Cadillac touring car, you know, with the tunneau windshield in the back, a classic thing. It was a terrific piece of machinery. He parked outside the station on Grove Street. Everybody who walked past used to admire it. She thought I owned the car. She thought I was the guy. So she wrote me a little note saying okay. When I called for her, I was on foot. I didn't have a car. I didn't even have a bicycle. That's how Shirley and I met.

But all of these things happened because of that one little key. It's so true of life, how everything can hinge on one little happening. The girl in the cage said "Why don't you come back in twenty-five minutes?" And I said, "What the heck, I'll go across to the Travelers building." Maybe if it had been a mile away, I wouldn't have gone. But it was right across the street. I walked in. They said, "Okay, go to work." Boom, the next day I went to work. They said that if you can pass the physical, you can go to work. I said, "What do you mean, physical? You have to be in good shape to get a radio announcing job? You have to fight your way into the studio?" This was the Travelers Insurance Company. They didn't want to hire anybody who was an invalid or going to die in a few days. The boss said, "If you can pass this, you can go to work tomorrow." That's how it all started. And that's why I feel I'm such a lucky guy.

Sandy Hale has been showing her photographs in group and individual exhibitions since 1978. In 1984, one of her photos was purchased by the State of Connecticut's Commission on the Arts. An invitational lecturer at Eastern Connecticut State University, in Willimantic, Connecticut, Sandy resides in Windham Center, Connecticut, with her husband and two children.

Jane Moskowitz and **Jane Gillard** are partners in Propaganda, their Mansfield Center, Connecticut, advertising agency. Having seven children between them, both Janes have counted on Bob's help for years to get their husbands, children and themselves on their way with a smile.

Arden Reardon, typesetter, is the owner of Keystrokes in Lenox, Massachusetts. She lived in Connecticut during her earlier years and has fond radio memories of Bob Steele.

Laurie Reardon is a graphic artist, born in Connecticut but transplanted to Massachusetts. She is the co-owner of photo/graphics.